home again

home again

ESSAYS AND MEMOIRS FROM INDIANA

EDITED BY

TOM WATSON AND JIM MCGARRAH

INDIANA HISTORICAL SOCIETY PRESS
INDIANAPOLIS 2006

Printed in the United States of America

This book is a publication of the
Indiana Historical Society Press
450 West Ohio Street
Indianapolis, Indiana 46202-3269 USA
www.indianahistory.org

Telephone orders 1–800–447–1830
Fax orders 317–234–0562
Online orders @ shop.indianahistory.org

The paper in this publication meets the minimum requirements of American National Standard for Information Sciences—Permanence of Paper for Printed Library Materials, ANSI Z39.48-1984.

Library of Congress Cataloging-in-Publication Data

Home again : essays and memoirs form Indiana / edited by Tom Watson and Jim McGarrah.
   p. cm.
  ISBN-13: 978-0-87195-198-4 (alk. paper)
  ISBN-10: 0-87195-198-3 (alk. paper)
   1. Indiana—Social life and customs—Anecdotes. 2. Indiana—Biography—Anecdotes.
I. Watson, Tom, 1949 Dec. 8– II. McGarrah, Jim, 1948–

F526.6.H66 2006
977.2—dc22   2006045776

INDIANA

In the town where I live women once built
P 47's in the same factories where men now
Build washing machines. I guess you could say

It's a town of some irony. Yet the smell
Of war effort is still strong here. Not far
Down the river from the moored, fake stern-wheeled

Party boat, are the sunken dry docks
Where they riveted together L.S.T.'s
For Normandy. And the bus station

Still breaks my heart—all late 30's
Science fiction, it touched down in a hum of neon
And everyone got off, rolled up their sleeves,

And went to work. I took a bus from there once,
For 50 dollars, and if you could blot out the video games,
You'd almost believe you were AWOL, or heading

For some genuine horror in the South Pacific.
It's a funny town. And I don't mean it's a place
"time forgot," just a place that has evacuated

Its self from time. It doesn't take responsibility
For its own history, and maybe they need to build
A monument or something, to commemorate what happened

To outdated aircraft and all the dead boys
Who flew them. We know what happened
To the women who built the planes,

They're doing the wash. Or their daughters are.
I watch them carefully in the Laundromats, talking
And laughing, sorting the colors from the whites,

While behind us
The sky goes off forever.

Matthew Graham
From 1946

Contents

SECTION ONE

A Cultivated State

Foreword

THIRTEEN WAYS OF LOOKING at the volume *Home Again*, edited by Tom Watson and Jim McGarrah:

1. "I am here." These three words, according to Nobel laureate Creslaw Milosz, "contain all that can be said." A book about Indiana by twenty-two different authors can reasonably be said to have something to do with that thought. What is a book about a smallish, midwestern state about if not how, to each of its authors, he or she is "here." Even the word "Hoosier," whose origin is unknown, translates easily into "Who's here."

2. On reflection, you might add qualifications such as "I am still here" or "Once I was there, and now I am here," but the differences are relatively minor. And really, says Milosz, you can only write about your own time and place—having been given no other. "This," he says, "is all very fundamental, but, after all, the science of life depends on the gradual discovery of fundamental truths."

3. Such statements are not, however, quite as simple as they seem. For one thing, they mix the subjective with the objective. They raise issues such as "Who Is 'I'?" and "Where is 'here'?" (also "Who wants to know?"). On the subject side, the "I" side, things become rapidly rhetorical: "What image of himself or herself does 'I' wish to present?" And "Is that image commensurate with the person 'I' actually is?" And "Of what does he or she wish to persuade us?" Then too, they raise

all kinds of questions about context: "What social, ethnic, national, regional, gender, religious, generational, historical, educational, racial perspective, etc. does 'I' represent?" and "What habits of speech or written communication, what textual conventions, are in evidence in his or her presentation?" Suddenly, what seemed like a fairly straightforward observation—"I am here"—seems overwhelming and impossible to ascertain. Such are the problems of our highly (some say "overly") intellectualized age. On the object side, the "What do you mean by 'here'?" side, similar questions abound.

4. Let's deal with the title, "Back Home Again." The phrase is from a song, "Indiana," written in 1917 by James F. Hanley, lyrics by Ballard Mac-Donald, the opening line of which is, "Back home again in Indiana." Recently on NPR (May 23, 2003) commentator Bob Cook pointed out that it was so well known because it has been sung for thirty-five years by Jim Nabors (not a Hoosier) prior to the Indianapolis 500-Mile Race to not only the more than three hundred thousand people who attend the race each year but also to the untold millions who hear it over the radio or on television. The NPR story was at pains to point out the homeliness and sentimentality of Nabors's rendition mostly by observing that the tune has had a lively history not only among the unwashed and ordinary but also the sophisticated and the cognoscenti.

5. Detached from its origins in song, the title seems equally sentimental. "Home" has resonances of unabashed love mixed with feelings of anxiety and fear such as attend our earliest beginnings. "Back" and "Again" both imply all those returns and reunions that haunt and plague our attempts at adult life. Redundancy only makes these questionable feelings stronger.

6. In Kentucky "Back Home" would be stated as "Down Home" or perhaps "Back Down Home," although the sentiments are similar. I don't know why in Kentucky northerliness, as a direction, means distance from one's roots.

7. Sentimental attachments notwithstanding, the kernel in the title's message is nonetheless mysterious. Will this book allow us to return back home, again, in thought and imagination? Will it allow us to recover *lost youth*? The prospect is horrifying.

8. Will it allow the writers through their personal narratives to experience such a return? But then what about those writers whose narra-

tives recount the experience of coming to Indiana for the first time, sometimes from places far away, followed by a stay of indeterminate duration? Perhaps the only return for them is an anticipated future return. Hmm.

9. I am aware of certain, shall we say, imbalances in the text. Some of these writers seem to imply that the essence of being a Hoosier lies in small-town, rural values and attitudes (and basketball), belying the fact that it is and has been a fair-sized industrial state with a history of manufacturing, union organizing, and even socialism. (Are Hoosiers proud or ashamed of Eugene V. Debs?) Hummers are built in Mishawaka, Toyotas in Princeton, and Subarus in Lafayette. Indeed, at a recent summit held by the Indiana Humanities Council, a principal speaker said Indiana should give up its dreams of becoming a high-tech, med-tech corridor and stick to what it knows. What he meant was not soybeans and corn but rather manufacturing, especially of recreational vehicles.

10. Others paint an idyllic picture of a place that engenders not only traditional values but also a surprising amount of political, cultural, and artistic refinement and understanding, having given to the world such people as Hoagy Carmichael, Paul Dresser, Cole Porter, Gene Stratton-Porter, John Mellencamp, and Kurt Vonnegut, as well as Halston and Bill Blass. The implication is that Indiana is, indeed, a good place to be from. It is tempting to add Abraham Lincoln, who spent his formative years in Indiana before moving to Illinois, to this list. Was Abe an early example of the brain drain that afflicts us still? But the question, then as now, seems to be if Indiana is so great, why leave?

11. One commodity in which Hoosiers excel is the creation of narratives. These come in both official and unofficial forms. An example of an official narrative is the tagline on our license plate, "Crossroads of America," implying centrality. It used to be "Wander Indiana," implying aimlessness.

12. Unofficial narratives include all the vast collection of stories, novels, poems, plays, songs, biographies, reminiscences, lies, fibs, stretchers, and so forth that exist from before statehood in 1816 down to the present. These include the creations of writers from our golden past—James Whitcomb Riley, Meredith Nicholson, George Ade, Lew Wallace, Charles Major, and Edward Eggleston—and others who are

not so golden such as one of my favorites, James Buchanan Elmore, the bard of Alamo (Indiana). They also include the essays in the current book, itself a work that builds on predecessors such as *Where We Live: Essays about Indiana*, edited by David Hoppe and published by Indiana University Press in 1989.

13. The only genuinely mystical experience I ever had was one day on First Avenue in Evansville when it came to me in a flash that none of these red-brick buildings, these factories, houses, and churches, *had* to be there. They were merely an idea of old Europe or an expression of individual or collective willpower (if not to say greed) that caused some settlers to plunk themselves down on the banks of the Ohio, where it was momentarily convenient to do a little business, make a little stir or, as it happens, swap some stories. The relationship between selfish and collective enterprise and storytelling should not be so surprising after all. Stories grant us permission to say who we are (to say "I am here") and to be who we want to be. All told (!) Indiana is a bookish place, where storytellers populate what was once a wilderness (and may be a wilderness still) with tales of their dreams and of their passing. *Home Again* is another noble effort in that noble cause.

Tom Wilhelmus

Introduction

WITH ALL DUE RESPECT to Thomas Wolfe, going home again has more to do with renewal than nostalgia, especially in the Midwest. Sure, we pretend not to notice the encroachment upon the farmland of the "outstanding in the field" homes developers have seen fit to erect. We look past the fast-food joints and box stores that have replaced the mom-and-pop eateries and shops. We're all very much aware that things will never be the same, no matter how nostalgic the music from the local classic rock station that drifts through the car. We go home, not to reclaim some lost energy from youth or indulge ourselves in memories of the way things used to be, but rather because, simply, we *know* the Midwest. More particularly, as this anthology proves, we *know* La Porte, *know* Bloomington, Evansville, Indianapolis, Gary, East Lansing, Anderson, Patoka, Fort Branch, and a dozen more little cow patches off the shoulders of Highways 41 and 67 and Route 50. We understand that, just as trees are nourished and renewed through their roots, so is the human spirit.

Nothing is unusual about feeling a connection with the place where we grew up. Most people have the roots of their hometowns firmly entrenched and entangled in the very fiber of their beings. Like the roots on impacted wisdom teeth, they are very difficult and painful to remove. However, there seems to be an intrinsic pull toward Indiana from all geographical extremities in the rest of the country that transcends ordinary longings for home. Perhaps this state is to the United States what the heart is to the body. Everything that is the essence of what keeps us alive flows to and from this center, drawn in and pumped out to replenish and reinvigorate all the other parts. Many of the essays in this anthology will be concerned with that elemental motion, circulation to and from, and back to Indiana, as a way to survive in some instances and, in others, as a way to re-create the self.

We didn't necessarily plan it that way. However, what we found out as we began collecting the material was that many of our literary friends who currently live, or have lived, in this heartland had undergone the same catharsis we had. With that knowledge, the theme of being home again in Indiana emerged.

It isn't an original theme. The opening line of one of James F. Hanley's best-loved songs is "Back home again in Indiana, where the trees and wildflowers bloom." Mark Twain, in one of his famous essays involving moral courage and civic virtue, speaks of the strong-hearted Sheriff Beloat, who quelled the lynching of an African American in none other than Princeton, Indiana, in the nineteenth century. Now the fact that a lynching was about to take place in Indiana, as they already had in many other states in the Midwest and the South following the Civil War, isn't necessarily related to the theme of this anthology, but the attitude of Beloat certainly is. Many of these essays will speak to that very idea of moral courage and bravery exhibited by Beloat, in different circumstances perhaps, but with the same desire to find the center and the goodness of humanity, in both geography and in virtue.

At first, we envisioned a collection that would celebrate Indiana as the Crossroads of America, a place where there are both steel mills and millponds, congested cities and cornfields, high-rises and microscopic hamlets. We sought to showcase the excellent writing talents of Hoosier writers. *Home Again* would be about Indiana natives writing about their home state.

What we discovered while amassing the selections in this book was something larger and vastly more important than any mere catalog of essays reflecting upon Indiana from diverse points of view. We found we had tapped into themes relating to traditional American values like home, family, security, and the protestant ethic. We found our colleagues who submitted work to us wrote about quests for a better life, a life rooted in Indiana. We found the essays spoke about staying in Indiana to continue that quest, moving to Indiana in following that quest, or moving back to Indiana to bring closure to it.

* * * *

Of course, "home" has many different connotations, and this anthology explores the diversity of what being "home" in Indiana means to some. Alyce Miller, in "How I Tried to Become a Hoosier," discusses her attempt to become a Hoosier after having moved to Indiana from California; Michael Martone, in "Country Roads Lined with Running Fences," talks about place affecting the sense of "home"; Kurt Vonnegut, in "To Be a Native Middle Westerner," describes the wonder an inhabitant of the heartland feels; and Michele Gondi, in "The Redneck Gift," reflects upon finding "home" in Mount Vernon after moving from her native Argentina. Scott Russell Sanders discusses the lives of quarry workers in his "Doorways into the Depths," and Susan Neville, in her "Quake," reflects upon life in New Harmony. The tone of the anthology ranges from the pastoral, as in Scott Saalman's dreamlike account of his work with his grandfather in "Cider Days," to humorous yet scholarly, as in Rick Farrant's account of the history of the name for Indiana's residents, "Hunting for Hoosiers." Melanie Culbertson provides a hilarious social narrative, "Sleeping on Cowpatties and Other Hoosier Dating Rituals," and Ed Breen finds solace along a northern Indiana creek in "A Country Walk." In other essays we see the authors talk about the Amish, hardware stores, crystal clear lakes, Bobby Knight, unlocked doors, and urban sprawl.

* * * *

This book taught us valuable lessons about what we mean when we say we are home again. We hope readers will learn something important when they read it as well.

Carlos Fuentes said, "Bad books are about things the writer already knew before he wrote them." As we have learned much in compiling this anthology, likewise, we hope readers of *Back Home Again* will explore their own sense of what "home" means to them and discover more about the life quest upon which they have embarked. For those who have decided Indiana is the center of their known universe, we hope they will find assurance here that they have got to the heart of the matter metaphorically and physically in the Crossroads State. We hope our nonnative readers will include Indiana in their quest, for to be in Indiana, if only for the first time, it is to be truly home again.

Tom Watson and Jim McGarrah, editors

Acknowledgments

WE WISH TO THANK Sherrianne Standley, Vice President for Advancement at the University of Southern Indiana, the many fine writers who contributed essays to this book, the editorial staff at the Indiana Historical Society, and especially, Tam Bagby for her support and encouragement.

Tom Watson
Jim McGarrah

A Cultivated State

Courtesy of Ed Breen

"Tennui musam meditmaur avena—We cultivate literature upon a little oatmeal."

Reverend Sydney Smith

Hunting for Hoosiers

THERE IS SOMETHING about this place called Indiana that keeps drawing me back for one more look, one more run at taking in all its splendors and, at the same time, tolerating its considerable flaws. Something that is so strong, it has lured me here twice, once from Montana for a newspaper job in Hammond in 1976, and later circuitously from Colorado for another newspaper job in Fort Wayne in 1996.

Invariably, I've been asked: "How could you leave Montana?" "How could you leave Colorado?" Such queries of utter astonishment are followed by ancillary questions: "Why Hammond?" "Why Fort Wayne?" And what does one say? How does a person justify leaving a pristine, mountain-studded frontier where the dawn and dusk of each day are as close to heaven as one can get and trading such marvels for a largely flatland territory where residents consider knobs synonymous with mountains and who, until recently, intimated somewhat mistakenly that Indiana was the home of a God cloaked in the red-sweater guise of former Indiana University basketball coach Bob Knight?

How indeed?

The simplest, most honest answer I've been able to give people is that I came looking for work. But having spent more than a fifth of my life and more than a third of my professional career in Indiana, it occurred to me, gradually, that there must be something else to this recurring attraction. And finally I think I've stumbled upon it, albeit accidentally, in the quest to answer Indiana's most perplexing question.

Imperfection. I am attracted to people and places that offer rich textures of humanity—in all their glories and with all their faults.

Places where people, God love them, foster occasional good humor and more frequently pride, even if both are sometimes misplaced.

Places like Indiana, where the list of native and resident luminaries, distinguished as it generally is, must demand a measure of humor along with the pride: former vice president Dan Quayle, who couldn't spell potato; Johnny Appleseed (a.k.a. John Chapman), who was an oddball in his time if there ever was one; popcorn king Orville Redenbacher, whose name and countenance must surely have been the source of quips elsewhere in this great land; and the aforementioned Knight, whose infamous tirades could not have been stomached without some semblance of humor.

Indiana has also celebrated its good nature by sending into the world other celebrities whose business it is to make people laugh: David Letterman, Red Skelton, "Garfield's" Jim Davis, and James Whitcomb Riley, among them.

And Indiana continues to illustrate its humor and pride by stubbornly hanging on to the moniker by which its residents are known ("Hoosiers"), even if no one knows where the term comes from or what it truly means.

Therein lies the perplexing question for the ages—and its odd juxtaposition with nobility.

It's in the Webster's dictionary, this word—"Hoosier: A native or inhabitant of Indiana." It's also in the local phone book; in Allen County alone, there are nearly thirty references to businesses bearing the title, from food supply companies to landscapers to mortgage consultants. It's even the nickname of Indiana University's athletic teams, though the teams have largely labored without a mascot. (For short stretches, the mascot was either a bison or a "Hoosier Guy" bedecked in a cowboy hat and bearing a block of a jaw.)

Poor Indianans. How hard it must be envisioning a mascot to represent a term so shrouded in mystery, not only among scholars but also the masses at large.

* * * *

Take, for instance, the twenty-one-year-old green-eyed, flaxen-haired Hooters waitress who rests an elbow on a high-topped table before her and leans ever so slightly to her left.

"What is a Hoosier?" she asks, repeating the question.

She pauses for several seconds, a tepid, lost-in-thought grin on her face. Then she answers.

"An Indiana University basketball lover," she says, smiling more broadly.

"Good answer," pipes in someone nearby, apparently agreeing that it's as sound a response as any.

The question that follows—the one about the origin of the word "Hoosier"— thoroughly befuddles her, though.

"Oh shoot," she says. "I learned that a long time ago. But I don't know, honey. I don't know."

Chances are she never knew—because no one has.

* * * *

"It's a question that's been trying the patience of many historians for a long time," says Ray Boomhower, managing editor of the Indiana Historical Society's *Traces* magazine.

He should know. He's had a front row seat to the sundry theories—some of them serious, some of them in jest—proffered over the years by amateur and enlightened sleuths alike.

He's been privy to the notions which are pure folly, like the lingering folk-lore that nineteenth-century neighbors, upon approaching a house, would announce themselves with a query: "Who's yere?"

Or poet Riley's playful proposition that the early settlers "were vicious fighters . . . [and] frequently bit off noses and ears. This happened so often that a settler coming into the barroom after a fight would see an ear on the floor and ask, 'Whose ear?'"

Or that Indiana rivermen were called "hushers" because they were adept at quashing adversaries, and that the word later evolved to "Hoosiers."

Boomhower's also heard, read, and written about the more likely explanations—one new and one nearly a century old. Both portend rather negative connotations of the term and suggest the word was first used in the South, then crept north.

William D. Piersen, a professor of history at Fisk University in Nashville, Tennessee, provides the most recent hypothesis. He suggests the word comes from illiterate black evangelist Harry Hoosier, a traveling Methodist minister of some note in the late eighteenth century.

Piersen writes in the *Indiana Magazine of History*: "Throughout the southern frontier Methodists were not only slighted as unsophisticated and unlettered but they were also denigrated for calling into question the virtues of racial slavery. . . . Therefore, it does not seem at all unlikely that Methodists and then other rustics of the backcountry could have been called 'Hoosiers'—disciples of the illiterate black exhorter Harry Hoosier—as a term of opprobrium and derision."

Shortly after the turn of the twentieth century, journalist and historian Jacob Piatt Dunn came up with another conclusion—that the word, in some fashion, derived from the Cumberland, England, dialect and, at the time, could have meant anything from unusually large to hill-dwellers to uncouth country bumpkins.

Most scholars seem to hail Dunn's take on the subject, but they don't entirely discount Piersen's spin, either. The only thing they seem to truly agree on is that the word "Hoosier" was first widely recognized in Indiana around 1830 with the publication of a poem by John Finley titled "The Hoosier's Nest." Two paintings based on the poem later reinforced the word.

What's curious is that, somehow, Hoosiers became a prideful rallying cry for the young state, which entered the union in 1816 with just 70,000 inhabitants. More than half the land was still possessed by Indians then, says *The History and Topography of the United States*, published in 1834. Vincennes—not Indianapolis, Fort Wayne, Gary, or Evansville—was the largest town in the state. The major local produce were corn, rye, oats, barley, buckwheat, potatoes, pulse, beef, pork, butter, whiskey, and peach brandy. Well-timbered woodlands, wide-open prairies, rambling rivers, and soggy bottoms comprised the landscape.

* * * *

James H. Madison, a professor of history at Indiana University who has pondered the origin of the state's moniker for more than thirty years as both a student and educator, says Indiana's infancy may explain why Hoosiers became an accepted term.

"It was," he says, "a quest for identity because it was a relatively new state and people wanted to assert Indiana in America. [Being an Indiana resident] was a badge of honor, a badge of pride."

Why such a dubious term has managed to hang around for so long is another matter. It is, I suppose, marginally understandable that native Hoosiers gladly attach themselves to such a peculiar identity. They've never known anything else. But it seems—on the surface of it, anyway—to make little sense when people like myself, with no known ancestry in Indiana and possessing allegiances to other state brandings, accept the new title so readily.

It could have just as well "faded away and . . . be lost," Madison observes. "Maybe the IU Hoosiers would have become the Cougars."

Or the Colts or the Jaguars, for that matter. Who knows?

* * * *

Take the thirty-five-year-old boyish-looking man and his effervescent wife sitting in Row 28, Section 136, Seats 1 and 2 inside the capital city's RCA Dome.

It's the third quarter of a game between pro football's Indianapolis Colts and Jacksonville Jaguars.

The man is a native of Beech Grove, Indiana, and he's had the season-ticket holder seats since 1984.

It's his job to know Indiana. After all, he owns a relocation company and he helps newcomers settle in the Hoosier State.

But he doesn't have an earthly clue where the word comes from or what it means, other than he knows he's a Hoosier and he's darn proud of it.

"I should know,'" he says.

Then again, about the only thing his clients are interested in talking about is Bob Knight, who doesn't even coach IU basketball anymore. He was unceremoniously banished to Texas Tech, where there is, incidentally, a mascot. The Masked Rider.

* * * *

Madison finds people's inability to explain the term amusing, especially when his university struggles to put a face to the name.

"It's just fun to watch people fool with it, go nuts with it, get frustrated with it," he says. "I think the fascination of the whole debate, which has gone on for more than a century now, is that it's going to continue to go on and that there's no answer, no convincing logical explanation."

And that likelihood, he and Boomhower say, is probably for the best. The mystique will keep people talking about Indiana.

For better or worse, but hopefully for the better, Madison says.

"It's very important for Hoosiers to assert it in a positive manner," he says defiantly. "Don't let the sons of bitches use it as a negative term."

Don't let them tarnish the legacies of the great Hoosier writers and lyricists like Ernie Pyle, Theodore Dreiser, Kurt Vonnegut, Booth Tarkington, George Ade, Gene Stratton-Porter, and Cole Porter; the accomplished athletes like Knute Rockne, Gil Hodges, Larry Bird, Oscar Robertson, and Jeff Gordon; the noted performers like The Jackson Five, Crystal Gayle, Carole Lombard, and James Dean; or the fearless innovators like aviator Wilbur Wright, jazz guitarist Wes Montgomery, television inventor Philo T. Farnsworth, and fashion designer Bill Blass.

Don't let them trample on the sweeping cinnamon sunsets; the glistening green waves of corn that seem to go on forever; the geese on the fly; the owl in the wood; or the sandstone gorges cut masterfully by water and wind into magnificent works of art.

Help them suspend, for the moment, the knowledge that Indiana has been home to the infamous as well as the famous. That outlaw John Dillinger once rumbled across its dusty roads, or that it has been, at various times, associated with factions of the Ku Klux Klan.

Show them the spirit of the state, which dwells in the myriad festivals that celebrate everything from heroes to heritage, the little towns bypassed by railroad and highway that continue to flourish because they've cultivated a sense of community, and the sprawling factories that employ only the hardiest of men and women.

Above all, don't let the naysayers suggest the word Hoosier must have been dreamt up by a bunch of uneducated, humorless yahoos from the back forty. That might be the case. Then again, it probably doesn't matter anymore.

* * * *

Take the blond-haired, big-toothed, ten-year-old fifth-grader inspecting books with his mother at a Barnes and Noble.

He's boiled all the highfalutin, complicated conjecture down to a simple science.

A Hoosier, he says, is "an Indiana person."

And the origin of the word? Well, he says, that's easy.

"It comes from the guy who made it up."

I like that answer best. It provides the freedom to accept Indiana for what it is. Alternately pristine and tarnished, from the rural ambience of blue skies and rolling hills in the south to the smoke-choked, steel-milling shorelines of Lake Michigan in the north. At once sophisticated and primitive, from the university towns employing articulate people of the highest intellect to the places in between where any tense will do. Always changing and always staying the same.

This is my Indiana and, for better or worse, I am finally back home again. And if you should choose to call me a Hoosier, I won't mind.

The label, I have come to discover, is a perfectly imperfect word for a beautifully imperfect state.

What's in a Name?

MY MOTHER HAS the kind of maiden name I always wanted, a name I coveted, a name that was long, hard to pronounce, European, and decidedly "other." Many women learn very early that they will probably lose their names when they marry, so it goes without saying that if you know you will lose something, you don't get very attached to it. I can't help but wonder sometimes if my mother found tremendous relief when she married and forfeited her maiden name: Engel de Janosi.

It's a beautiful, terrible name. The *de* means *of*, and the word *Engel* means *angel* as in the angels of Janosi. Janosi is a house that no longer stands in a town that does not exist in Hungary, which is barely still a country.

My mother was meant to inherit a palace with her name, but you can't smuggle that kind of property across borders and into a new country.

The angels of Janosi were aristocrats who also happened to be Jewish, a fact I had to find out for myself because my mother, who was and always has been Catholic, never spoke of the angels in her family. After my grandfather died, I read his memoir and his father's memoir. My grandfather wrote about all the important people he knew such as Sigmund Freud and Henrik Ibsen. He mentions my mother two times in his memoir. He never mentions my sister or my father or me. I think to him we did not exist, so why name us?

My grandfather's father, Josef Engel de Janosi, wrote that he was writing only for his descendants. He tells us about his love for his religion, his hard work during bad times, and his very successful parquet floor factory. He knew a lot about wood and how to get lumber from here to there. He wrote about his family (each of whom he named), his town, and his workers and how he built them a swimming pool and a temple.

They're all gone now—the houses, the factories, the silver, the art, the pool, the temple, the people. Confiscated or blown up during two world wars. Hitler played a big role in the destruction of the angels.

The Nazis were a lot like the crusaders, taking out people, buildings, towns, even graveyards. We know now that their goal was not only to erase a people but also to erase their history, and to do that you've got to get rid of documents and names. Maybe more than any other group, they taught us the power of fire and the documentation of names.

I first read about the Engel de Janosi the summer after I married, when my husband and I moved into a rented farmhouse in Darmstadt, Indiana, which was, and still is, a German settlement. The house was small, but it had a big kitchen and it sat on top of a windy hill surrounded by pine trees and fields that alternated between corn, soybeans, and winter wheat. It was the most beautiful place we could imagine living, and I tried not to care that we rented from a family named Goebel.

German family names appear on almost every mailbox on the side of the road, and umlauts are engraved on practically every other gravestone in the cemeteries of Darmstadt, but still, it was a struggle to grow accustomed to living among the Schmidts, the Bucheles, the Kuhnes, and the Hohmers. Schoolchildren there learn and often speak German and not French, which is what I studied in school. My husband and I were temporary settlers in Darmstadt, and we laughed about our neighbors' odd habits of boarding up their windows in winter, losing the fantastic views and light but saving on heat. Even though we were renters and we knew we would eventually move, I had trouble with the place, even resented knowing that most of these families immigrated to the area in the 1820s when there was a rising tide of emigration from Germany. Even the name, Darmstadt, which most people pronounce in the correct, German way, *Darmshtadt,* made my skin—what can I say?—crawl.

According to the literature I've read, Hesse-Darmstadt is an agricultural area in southwestern Germany dotted by villages, deep forests, medieval towns, and castles. You've got the Rhine River to the west and the Main River to the east, and between these rivers, in the Hesse highlands, sits Darmstadt.

Darmstadt, Indiana, is a landlocked village with two railroads and an abundance of corn, wheat, soybean, pumpkin, and Christmas tree farms. Even though the current sign on the outskirts of Darmstadt says the town was formed in 1822, the land was purchased from the government as early as 1818. Darmstadt was probably named by an early settler and community leader, Michael Bauer, to honor his wife, Barbara, who came from Hesse-Darmstadt. Darmstadt officially became an incorporated village on July 2, 1973, the year of the United States energy crisis. In the summer of 1987 the Village Square shopping center was remodeled to look like a German village.

During our first years of marriage, living out there in Darmstadt, I was writing about one woman's first years of marriage and another woman who was trying to be something she was not—Jewish. It was odd and seemingly revolutionary to be researching and writing about the Sabbath, Rosh Hashanah, Sigmund Freud, and Hannah Arendt, then glance out the window to see a young, shirtless Goebel riding a John Deere tractor through the soybean fields.

I would go back to my books, thinking surely in this twentieth-century village, on this road called New Harmony, Goebels can coexist with Engels.

Two years before Indiana became a state, the Congress of Vienna was assembled in 1814, and there Germany, which was made up of 238 separate states, each with its own prince, was reduced to 38 states.

After the Congress, there was a great deal of unrest in Germany and in France, what with the population increasing, the scarcity of land, low wages, the uncertainty of governmental restrictions, and the fear of further strife. Meanwhile, land was cheap and plentiful in America, especially in the Midwest where an acre went for $1.25 in 1830. Many German farmers moved where they had friends and relatives in Missouri, Illinois, Ohio, Michigan, Wisconsin, and Indiana. Seventeen distinct German communities sprouted in southeastern Indiana, and many were in rural areas where there were already established farms. In *A History of Trinity Lutheran Church, Darmstadt,* Chester T. Behrman quotes one unnamed Evansville historian: "These people came with their habits of thrift, economy and pluck, well-recognized and inherent virtues of the Germanic race."

While living in Darmstadt, I attempted to get over my inherent "issues" with Germans, but all around me there were hints of anti-Semitism or simply anti-other-than-German. We drove a Volvo then, and I recall somebody once asking me why I owned a Swedish car. While walking once in Evansville near the university where I work, I saw a swastika chalked on the sidewalk. Nearby sat a gorgeous brick house with intricate designs in the brickwork, and even though the owner trained ivy to grow over it, one of the designs was a swastika, and

I knew, like everyone else in town, that the symbol was more Germanic than Nordic in meaning.

Still, our hilltop house and the village around it seemed to be isolated from all that was ugly in the world, even most economic and natural disasters. Neighbors told me that during the Depression, there was plenty of food and produce from the farms and no family went hungry. Darmstadt sits on higher ground, so, unlike Evansville, it missed the flood of 1937.

Darmstadt was and still is so beautiful. There are hills there, and they really do roll. Winters were straight out of a Currier and Ives painting. Even horses and buggies passed our house from a nearby Amish community. In the spring we could smell tortillas and taco shells cooking at the Azteca Milling Company, and from where we sat perched high up on our hill, we could watch trains go by three or four times a day. All year round you could get a dozen fresh brown eggs for seventy-five cents. In the summer big black and yellow butterflies fluttered all along the side of the road, and while the oil well moved up and down in the front yard, we could hear the machines drying the corn. In the fall, when we saw the sun coming up from our bedroom window, the plowed fields were so flat and vast, we thought for a moment we were near some wide, sandy beach. Even thunderstorms were beautiful. We sat on the porch, watching them come in from the distance.

I wish I could write a valentine to Darmstadt without any hesitations or discomfort.

In the course of three years out there, my husband and I finished a book and a movie between us. Now we live on a street named after Samual Bayard, an Evansville banker whose father was French. Some years we go to the Volkfest, where some of the people wear chicken hats or paper lederhosen because August in southern Indiana is too hot for leather. At Christmas concerts, I can even sing "Stille Nacht" and "O Tannenbaum" without flinching, mainly because they are beautiful songs, but still, I must confess to some degree of pleasure when I learned that the German newspaper, *The Democrat,* folded.

I know now that, like names, facts, information, families, towns, and countries can sometimes disappear, get ignored, or even buried over time. I know that 22 percent of adults think it might be possible that the Holocaust never happened. I know that the farmers in Darmstadt use tons of fertilizers, and it doesn't seem coincidental that Darmstadt has an unspoken but high rate of breast cancer. I know that buried beneath many fertile, rolling fields lies a certain degree of danger.

When I was born my mother loaded me up with Christian, Anglo-Saxon names, and even though I was never confirmed, she went ahead and tacked on a confirmation name long before I was of age so that I would be "safe." She loved that I was her blond, Catholic American daughter. No one could get me. So of course, when my son was born, I stuck my mother's maiden name into his middle name. She is the last Engel de Janosi and I did not want the name to die with her.

I could not name a town, but I had a son. And behold, there he is, the last angel: James Raymond Engel de Janosi O'Connor running across the room in his superman cape.

There is power in a name. At the end of "Easter 1916," W. B. Yeats lists the names of the men who died for their motherland. When you read that poem out loud, you have to pause at each name. You have to. The men died, but their names did not. Each name is a poem. Each name will make you weep.

I did not inherit a palace. I know very little about wood. But I know the power of anger, hatred, words, and names. And my son, he has my mother's maiden name.

Quake

December 3, 1990

I'M SITTING ON A BALCONY in New Harmony, Indiana, waiting for the end of the world.

I don't mind the wait. Every sixty years the sun and the moon battle for the earth's affections, and the body of the earth turns liquid and rolls. Earth tides, they're called, and everyone in the Midwest knows about them now. Something strange and unsettling in the solid earth we've counted on. We live on one of the world's largest fault lines, and most of our lives we weren't even aware of it. Some prophet has predicted that the tide will cause the fault to shift on this very day, and because we're only ten years away from the new millennium, something in us longs for the explosion.

Blow it all up, get rid of it: all the plastic pens and razors, and the World of Dinettes that sold us the one-hundred-dollar chairs that fell apart in one year. Blow up the immense shopping desert with the acres of stone lots and tall mercury lights like drooping flowers and all the brand-new vapory objects that pack the stores so tightly it makes us dizzy to walk through them. Blow up the church where we sit without fervor on Sunday, listening to announcements about the sidewalk fund, and the chaos of strip malls where it's impossible to walk from Toys R Us to Children's Palace one hundred yards away, and it takes an hour to drive through a confused tangle of unplanned traffic lights and roadways to the Kmart where last year a five-year-old girl from my neighborhood reached for a silver tube of toothpaste on a shelf and it blew off her hand. I put my own children in a metal shopping cart now like a cage, and I pray they won't reach their hands outside of it.

Because I've lived in the suburbs of Indianapolis all my life and I remember the forest of one-hundred-year-old beech trees that was cut to make that chaos, and because when I wake up in the middle of the night in the same neighborhood I lived in as a child, the sky isn't dark and crisp and starry, but this weird half-mystical shade of orange-gray-violet, when I heard about the earthquake, I ran hell-bent out of my township, down through the detritus of the city's spinning—past Auto Parts and Used Auto Parts and then old tires submerged in winter field, past rows of hay huddled under black trash bags. I ran from my own anger, down to where the earthquake map in the paper was shaded, to where I could feel it if it goes. In 1823 a prophet brought a group of people here from Germany to wait for the end of the world. The earthquake, if it comes, won't be just some minor trembling that shakes the curio cabinet here, and the Harmonists who've been waiting first in line, folded into the ground like egg whites for one hundred years, will shiver: hush, maybe this is it, what we've been waiting for, new life, our chance to rise. So I sit on a balcony overlooking Paul Tillich's grave, waiting with them for the end of everything.

It doesn't come. I try to meditate on important things. Instead, I think about local gossip, some scandalous reason that Tillich is buried here and the Harmonist granary across the street has never been restored. I think it has something to do with the IU calliope. I can't remember the story, and anyway it's probably not true. I stretch and drink coffee and wonder why I am so shallow even on earthquake day. I put my feet up on the balcony. The day is unseasonably warm, the climate turned strange, the globe a candled egg.

Wild geese rise up from the woods behind the Benedictine chapel. They have difficulty forming a V; one goose moves out in front and then another. The others have no idea which one to follow. Is that a sign? Do geese get confused before earthquakes? Supposedly, cats run away; that's part of the mythology. Keep your eyes on the want ads in the paper. I decided that I need a paper.

I walk downstairs and head toward town, past the log houses, the Roofless Church. I see the granary behind a gate. Private residence, the sign says. Things like that can't matter when you're waiting for the end of the world, so I walk in.

It's one of the largest barns I've ever seen—stone and log windows, the whole thing shaped like a loaf of bread. It's where the Harmonists stored hay for the millennium. The barn is covered with dead foliage like tangled hair, two cats sitting in the chink of light that's opened by a boarded-up window; maybe they've run away. I try to look inside. Rotted wood and fallen rafters, an expanse of dark like a cathedral, dusky light from windows high up. I walk around the corner of the barn, over to Robert Dale Owen's mad scientist laboratory, a weird Victorian structure with turrets like witches' caps, a metal fish twisting overhead. There were two different utopias here. It was only the first group who waited for the end of the world. The Owenites bought the whole town when it didn't happen and the Harmonists began revising their predictions. If the Harmonists thought that human beings were angels—Gabriel, it's said, even left his footprint in a stone above the Wabash—the Owenites thought they were machines. They were the ones who mapped and classified every inch of this wilderness, the ones who brought in the abstract and the rational. Make the perfect world, they thought, and you create a perfect human being. Strangely, though, it was the spiritual Harmonists who created the buildings that still stand, a simple beauty and order in the life they made, much like the Shakers. It was the rational Owenites who built very little, and when they did, created this wacky laboratory. Toward the end of his life, Owen decided the spirit was so completely disconnected from the body that he turned to séances, the air so thick with spooky spirits that he could hardly walk outside.

The wall of the granary on the laboratory side is covered with trumpet vine, hard, dried bean pods like the beaks of brown yammering toucans. I break a pod from the vine and put it in my pocket. The pods shake in the wind and it sounds like applause; the fish on the laboratory spins and spins.

I leave through the gate and head into town. I realize that I'll spend the very last day in the world shopping, the way we celebrate holidays in the suburbs. Labor Day Sale. Memorial Day Sale. After Thanksgiving, Pre-Christmas Sale. Armageddon Day Clearance, everything half off, take it with you. I try to talk to people about the earthquake, looking for a true believer, but only the agnostics are out.

A woman sits in a bookstore putting all the change from the church Sunday school into paper rolls, her finger stuck down inside a roll like one of those Chinese puzzles. "It's old people and children that are worried," she says to me, "people who don't have a thing to do. My mother's boxed up all her stuff and tied the water heater to the wall with cup hooks. My little boy's gone to stay with her; they can be scared together all day long."

A clerk with dangling paper-clippy-looking earrings overhears us. "It's not just old people," she says. "My insurance agent boxed all his stuff up and spent the night in his motor home. I'd be afraid the thing would topple over."

I tell her I talked to an insurance agent before I came down here, one from Anderson who had to hire three extra people to write up earthquake riders on policies even though Anderson's supposedly on a different plate. "You're as safe from this fault in Anderson," I say, "as you would be in Paris."

I buy books for my kids and a newspaper, head out the door. I check the sky, feel my feet on the sidewalk. Is that a rumble? Is everything solid? I put my hand on the cold stone building.

Around the corner to a white house where they sell woven goods. I walk in. Cross-stitch pictures of lambs and bins of colored yarn; maybe I can find a scarf for my brother. He can wear it in January if the weather turns cold enough. January? Yes, I think. January. If I really believed in this prediction, I wouldn't be here. I would have gathered up everyone I love and headed for an open field.

An old woman with short bowl-cut gray hair sits behind a floor loom. National Public Radio is on louder than any rock station. Something crashing and dissonant, the wood loom clacks like the dried trumpet vine on the granary.

"I'm not afraid of no earthquake," she says. "You talk about Kentuckians," she says, "but we're ignorant here, that's all." Hoosiers—damn ignorant—clack crash, the loom, the radio's percussion.

I try a purple shawl on over my coat, and it turns me into an old woman immediately. Last night in the restaurant, two old women with rounded backs, their eyes inches away from the tablecloth when they sat down; they looked like the handles of two umbrellas hooked over the table's edge. I pull the shawl around me, turn away from the mirror. I'm trying on old age to see how it feels.

"Ignorant," the woman says, "because they've never been out of the state in their lives"—clack crash—"never farther than Evansville, some of them, like my son's wife, they're divorced now, I wouldn't have said ignorant while she was married to him, but the week my son wanted to take her on a vacation to Dallas, my ignorant daughter-in-law said it was too far away, and that was the week she moved out with the baby and the furniture."

"Ignorant"—clack crash—"just damn ignorant."

Another old woman in jeans and a red stocking cap comes in the back door, puts down a sack. There are three of us now. I hunch over, move toward the loom.

"We get the baby every eight days," the weaver says, "and they're beating her."

"Who's they?" the woman in the red cap says.

"How awful," I say.

"They're beating her"—clack crash—"and we can't prove it."

"Scars are being formed there," the other woman says.

"Every eight days then Wednesday, Thursday, Friday, Saturday, Sunday, and the baby cries when we try to take her back to her mother."

"Pillar to post," the other woman says, "lifetime scars are being formed there."

The weaver slams the shuttle through the loom. "We don't know who's beating her," she says, "maybe the day care, we can't prove it."

"Are there bruises?" the other woman says.

"No," the weaver says, "but she cries too hard for no reason."

"Scars you can't see," the other woman says, "scars being formed there."

I put the shawl back on the wire and straighten my back.

"I've been to Hawaii," the weaver says, "to my sister's house in California. An earthquake in California, they just look up and go on, not like here."

"Something needs to shake us up," she says.

"Shake, rattle, and roll," her friend says.

"You like the shawl?" the weaver says to me. "I didn't mean," she says, with a crash, the beater bar shoving the threads so tight they will never unravel, "to tell you a horror story on earthquake day."

I walk outside. Everything is still the way it was, but different. There are earthquake stories everywhere. I walk down the street to the Main Street Café, walk in, sit down. Three more old women in a booth next to mine. A man in a John Deere hat walks by. There are all these tired graying faces, but this man's face is a candle. "There were tremors," he says to the table of women, "tremors at 10:30." Of course! Everyone nods, revisionist history. So that's what it was, we think, the sound I heard—not a truck going by on the highway, not a man moving furniture in the apartment upstairs, not a woman taking out her troubles on a loom. It wasn't one of my spells, I hear a woman say to a friend, right about then it was I leaned into the truck and started hoping that someone would come along and save me. Tremors! Our new lives can begin now, all fresh, everything bad sloughed off like water through a colander.

"You from around here?" one of the women at the booth says to me, just like you would expect her to. "No," I say, "I'm staying at the inn." She tells me she lives in the green stucco house across the street, the one with the ceramic elves in the window, sure that I'd notice it. I assure her that I did notice it, and I tell myself I'll look for it when I leave. The last day in the world, and I've become a liar and a trespasser and a thief. There's no hope for me, none whatsoever. The woman is getting ready to go home and watch *Days of Our Lives*. I tell her I haven't liked it much since Doug and Julie left and Bo and Hope, and she says yeah, that Patch just got killed too, and I tell her I'm sorry, I didn't know.

"Remember when Patch was a bad guy?" I ask. And she says yes, that he was one of those good-looking bad guys that all the viewers fall in love with, so they turned him into a good guy, little by little. But not too good; he still had a wicked edge to him. It would come out when you least expected it. He died a good-guy death though, a hero.

I asked what's happening now—gossip, shopping, and soap operas are how we spend the last days of our own real lives—and she says they're all on an island and there's been an earthquake. They're holed up together in a building.

Not on earthquake day, I say to her, and she laughs and says, "You're not one of those who believes in earthquakes," as though it's something you need to have faith in, like God or love. And I laugh, say no, I'm not one of those. All of us out to lunch on this day are the ones who don't believe the earth is waiting to swallow us whole for our sins.

One of the woman's friends who lives up near Gary got in with a cult who moved into a church basement a few years ago, believing someone who said there was going to be a killer tornado. She thinks that all these earthquake believers are just as crazy. She tells me about another friend who's rigged up an outdoor generator and put a change of clothes and bottled water in both of her cars, with plans to live in whichever one survives the quake. The woman and her husband are both excited about it; it's given them something to talk about for months.

"I haven't done a thing to get ready for this earthquake," another woman says, as though it's something you have to prepare for, like Christmas.

"If I put all my food in one place," she says to me, "that's exactly the place the wall would cave in."

"You watch soap operas," I say to the women. "When a woman boxes up the baby and the furniture and moves away, what happens?"

"It depends," the ceramic elf woman says. "Sometimes the woman is happier, sometimes not. Sometimes the man is happier than the woman."

"And the baby?" I ask.

"Sometimes an accident," she says.

"Fire, drowning, hurricane, explosion," another woman says. "If the baby survives, she's moved all over the place. Everyone fights over her."

"Babies in soap operas never stay in one place long."

"Sometimes there's a kidnapping."

"Yes!" A woman in her husband's green thermal coat. "Some guy you've never even seen before comes in, claims he's the father, and grabs her. Some old lover of the wife—a Mafia guy sometimes, leader of a Virgin Islands cult."

"Everyone comes back together to save the baby," the elf woman says. "The baby's parents fall in love again."

"Months later there's a big wedding, a dress like Lady Di's. We all stay home to watch it and we cry and cry."

The thermal-coated woman says, "And at the last minute, the bride's brother runs in, his clothes all torn and dirty, holding the baby."

"The bride's brother or the groom's best friend?"

"No, the guy the bride left her husband for."

Yes, they all agree, that's best. And then?

"Bliss," one woman says. She wraps both hands around her bubbling Coke. "Bliss and bliss and bliss."

"For about a half a year," the elf woman says. "A half a year, then boom, crash, something happens to them. Or they go away for a while and the baby comes back replaced by a teenage actress and the whole thing starts all over."

"And in real life?" I ask.

"Who knows?" they say. Things happen, they agree, you can't predict. Things just go on and on and every once in a while there's an earthquake. The next day the sun comes up, you look around, and you see whether you're living your old life or a new one. It's exactly what I was afraid they'd say.

* * * *

The problem with this world is that things are so enmeshed. You can't predict a thing, good and evil so bound together that it's impossible, sometimes, to separate them. You try so hard for control and order, and you get disorder. You put your faith in science, and you see ghosts. How do you know how to live your life? The ground is always shifting underneath your feet.

Out here in the heart of the country we've rationalized every inch of earth—all the straight lines of highway and farm and township—but mystery and wildness still lie waiting deep inside every particle of the world, waiting to whirl or crack or ooze into our ordered lives, whether or not we've prepared for it. And the more we deny it, cover it up with concrete and lights, the tighter it crouches until it's as small and ordinary as a tube of toothpaste or as large as a crack in the foundations of the world, and we have to pay attention.

I leave New Harmony late in the afternoon, heading for the half-moon of my own confused township. The Harmonists still sleep. Another day almost gone, and still, they're waiting.

Halfway between New Harmony and Indianapolis, I pass two men butchering a deer. The deer hangs by its legs from a tree, its front hooves touching the earth. The men have hollowed the deer body, the ribs turned inward, something so graceful and terrifying in the curve of the animal and the curves of the branch it's hanging from, the men with their silver knives and orange caps, their jumpsuits the bronze cinnamon of the oak leaves, the dark flesh of the skinned deer mottled with fat, white like the bark of the sycamores in the woods behind them.

Byrd's *Mass for Three Voices*

IT WAS MIDWINTER in southern Indiana. Paul Hillier and the Pro Arte Singers were performing a concert of Renaissance music at the St. Meinrad Archabbey. It was a long drive on a Sunday afternoon, and I had many papers to grade—essays on Genesis for my humanities class, an unfinished novel of my own lying in wait for me. It was a dark day going out, with ice on the ponds and the road.

* * * *

In the abbey, the stained-glass windows were dark rubies, sapphires, and emeralds. There was no sunlight to penetrate them; they seemed animated by their own fires. The choir, nine young men, stood before the altar. The floor of the church was laid in colored marble triangles: blue, gold, rose, and white. They spread out from under the altar in dimming colors until the pattern was lost in gray marble waves. That is the world; the pattern lost, the waves smooth out as they get away from the impulse of the prime mover, itself unmoved, anchored in the altar.

The program, which had not been advertised, included William Byrd's *Mass for Three Voices*, one of my favorite pieces of music. The young men sang without accompaniment. The delay in the abbey is nine seconds. They began.

* * * *

The sound was startling. Each of the nine men had a beautiful, distinctive voice, but texture, resonance, vibrato disappeared in the blend. How many thousands of hours were required to achieve such unison, attack, dissolve, splitting off, doubling, symmetry? Perfection represented by the harmony of the spheres, according to Plato, according to Pythagoras; perfect intervals at which the planets are spaced, turn in their orbits, humming their perfect tone. One can predict the future by such disciplines: the obedient stars in the heavens, the dances of bees, the unfolding of petals. Such precision and balance of design must insure that all creatures by their very nature seek harmony.

* * * *

Driving home with cut fields on either side, I saw everywhere the beauty of symmetry and repetition—the frozen cornstalks and their shadows, power-line poles, standing regiments along the road. It was late afternoon; the sun had come out and the shadows were long. There were no other cars in view.

Suddenly a huge swirling flock of birds rose from the field on the left, crossing the highway before me. They were flying low, thousands of them, and at seventy miles an hour there was no way I could stop or miss them. Not yet, I thought—my kids are too young. In the last second before collision, I thought, how ironic that I would die, my windshield shattered, driving back alone from a concert of Byrd, killed by a flock of birds. What was my error?

I was going too fast on the slick road; I had driven far from home, alone, neglecting work, neglecting children, disdaining winter, for no purpose but my own pleasure. I was out of my depth. In fact I had left home long ago, left Los Angeles for the heartland. I was in retrograde; my family had reached the edge of the frontier, and I had turned back, looking for isolation, quiet, a clear tangent light, uncomplicated by distractions. I had underestimated everything: my self-sufficiency, simplicity, and especially nature.

But alas, there was no meaning to be construed from my choice twenty years past, or this day; it was not even bad luck. Just over.

As I entered the cloud, blacker than a midsummer thunderstorm, somehow the grackles veered away, flying before and behind me, not one of thousands touching my car. It was impossible, but as my car entered the crowd headlong, they changed direction, split off, maintaining all the while their perfect proportioned distances, like the wind moving through a field of wheat, a comb through hair, nine voices stretched across the octaves.

I pulled over to the side of the road. How could they achieve instantly what nine men spent years learning how to do? Humans delight in order and symmetry, but it is hard earned. How many hours spent on the field learning to march? If one bird had faltered, hundreds would have died, myself with them. Such things do not come naturally to us; it is easy to make an error in judgment.

* * * *

One winter morning my publisher put me on a train to Belfast.

"If there's a bomb on the line, they'll take you off," he said, "bring you in by van."

"Does it happen often?" I asked.

He shrugged. "Sure."

"Do you go to Belfast often?"

"Not really," he said. The last time he went, he'd had his taillights broken out at the border crossing. He said no more about it, but I knew Belfast was a long way from Dublin and that it must have been difficult to make it back before dark. He would have been stopped; there might have been trouble.

On the train I shared a compartment with three young men in suits. Engineering students, they said they were, on business in the north. "We're in the IRA," one said, and they laughed softly. We shared a packet of chocolates. Behind me an elderly priest read the *Irish Times*. As we passed the border I saw from the window the burnt roofs of farmhouses and barns. The Mourne Mountains were covered with blue mist.

When we stepped off the train in Belfast, the three young men were taken away by police.

In a cab on the way to the BBC, passing a high-rise office building, encircled by barbed wire, I heard running footsteps and machine-gun fire. The cab driver pointed out the famous window displays in Harrods: animated life-size Santas, elves, and reindeer. Armored tanks lined the decorated streets. At the BBC I passed through three bulletproof glass-vestibules, where I was frisked, identified, and assigned an escort. After the interview, I went Christmas shopping. At every threshold my bag was emptied, my coat and person scanned by guards with metal detectors and machine guns. There were no trash bins, no loitering, no stalls or carts with roasted chestnuts. On the streets people did not speak or look at one another.

Kyrie

That night, the train passed through Drogheda, some miles south of the border. A woman and her children were shot and killed while she bathed them. The cease-fire was broken.

Gloria

At midnight on the millennium there was peace on earth. We breathed easy, sitting before television between the Ohio River and the cut fields, far from the Eiffel Tower and the Parthenon, each in its glory, each in its time in jeopardy.

Credo

I drove into a cloud of grackles and in their wisdom they parted for me.

Hurtling toward their perfect symmetry, I had the right of way, the guarantee of no obstacles. This is America. I've read the book. According to Genesis, I have dominion over the creatures of the earth. I teach the subtleties of creation, nuances of power, shame, and imperfection, but in this slanting precise winter light I am out of sync.

* * * *

In Irish, the iridescent speckled black birds we call grackles are merlins. They nest inside gorse bushes, flying in and out between the needle-sharp thorns. In the middle ages, poets and singers were known by their speckled coats. In a pub in Ennystimon, I heard *sean-nós*, the old way, each song handed down from one singer to another for countless generations. We were in the Gaeltecht; it was prophesied that by the millennium there would be no native speakers of Irish. A woman in her eighties sang a long bawdy story, her voice like sandpaper, no tune left in it, then a young woman, her eyes shut with the song welling up from the ground, trills curling like wisps of smoke. The turn passed from singer to singer. When each came to the end of a verse, the others responded with a phrase unknown to me. I got the sense of it; *we're with you, go on, go on.* I realized that I had seen something like it in the margins of medieval epics, the *Chanson de Roland*, and the *Cantigas de Santa María*, though the footnotes called it gibberish. The crowd moved their hands in unison, keeping the song going, like they were weaving in air. There was no pause, no need for discussion, no rehearsal, no negotiations. The songs came spontaneously from the community of singers, like a flock of grackles lifting off from a field.

Then a man turned to me, to give me the song. "You'd like to recite something of your own," he said. I was ashamed. In my country it was not required; I had not learned. We have formal readings with a podium and sober audience, seated in rows. Such sharing was unnatural.

In the sixth century of our time the shepherd Caedmon left a gathering of shepherds when the harp was passed to him. He had nothing to sing, he said. That night he dreamt that a man came to him with a harp. "I sing about Creation," he said.

Sanctus

The birds veer off in perfect symmetry. If one person does not shoot another person, the cease-fire will not be broken.

Agnus Dei

We suffer a failure of synchronicity. Terrorism falls into our path. At the turn of the year, we are facing war. Our president longs for it. He looks everywhere for enemies. The world steps aside, but he turns again and again; he wants to collide.

There are many kinds of singing. We sing to march off to war, to make ourselves brave. In Caedmon's dream, he was told to sing of Creation. Can we be drilled in peace as well as war, if it does not come naturally to us?

Dona nobis pacem. Grant us peace. The mass is ended.

In the bleak midwinter, the birds settle down again in the field, in a clear and tangent light. Soon it will be dark. I must get home, to work.

MELANIE CULBERTSON

Sleeping on Cowpatties and Other Hoosier Dating Rituals

MY BOYFRIEND AND I trespass and camp on top of a round bare hill. Surrounded by open space, above the trees, we feel like we're being presented to the sky. We're careful with the flashlight, not wanting anyone to spy us. Cows usually graze here, but tonight they watch in the distance. We can't get comfortable enough to sleep because our bones rake against dried cowpatties underneath the tent. It's November, unusually warm for Indiana, but it grows so cold during the night that we roll ourselves up in our foam mattress. "Pigs in a blanket," we joke and laugh. At four in the morning, we rouse ourselves and rest our heads on the ground outside the tent door, looking up, our handkerchief-sized blanket tucked under our chins, our breath freezing the air. Crisp, bright stars are now covered by fog, making the sky look even colder and more surreal. Teeth chattering, we gawk at meteors, many of them, every few seconds—disappearing lines of orange ink. Come morning, we drink semiwarm hot chocolate from a thermos and watch the sun creep up and thaw the white, frozen ground.

When we camp at New Harmony State Park, northwest of Evansville, our plot is small and close to the other ones. While we enjoy a full moon, during the late evening and well into the night our uninhibited, Bud-belching neighbors blast our eardrums with Poison's "Every Rose Has Its Thorn," a song, I admit, for which I had an affection in the late eighties but have since outgrown. They don't play *any* other songs besides this one. I want to offer a nineties selection from my car, but I don't want to get them agitated. Once I finally drift off to sleep, I'm awakened when a fight between a couple in front of the nearby squat concrete restrooms almost turns violent. Obviously, at this park, whether the camping trip is good or bad depends on your neighbors and the state of the moon. At least they didn't howl.

These stories are a reminder of the common complaint that dating in Evansville and southwest Indiana is hard, particularly for single professionals. Hoosiers blame bad dates, bad meetings, bad whatever on Indiana: "There's not enough to do. There's no way to meet people." Evansville has been called among other things a "good place to be from" or "Indyucky." Southeast Indiana is associated with the Louisville region so much that the two are called Kentuckiana. Indianapolis and Bloomington form one area—the so-called cultured Indiana—and Fort Wayne forms another. Northwest Indiana is associated with Chicago. However, southwest Indiana is disconnected from big cities and has few defining characteristics; it's almost a no place in the middle of cornfields. The lack of a major highway linking it to central Indiana doesn't help. Sometimes when our ears perk up to "Funky Town" or Michael Jackson's "Beat It," commonly heard on Evansville radio, we feel stuck in a time warp. For entertainment, we're stuck with astronomical events and trespassing and such.

People who have the hardest time adjusting to the dating scene are outsiders, particularly ones who come from larger cities. As a single, thirty-year-old professor at the University of Evansville, I'm an outsider too, but I'm from Salyersville, in eastern Kentucky, where people practically skip dating and get hitched. If you want to go courting, you can (1) cruise the Pic Pac parking lot, (2) go to the movies and Pizza Hut in the next county over, or (3) go for the hot dogs-on-a-stick approach and build a fire in the woods closest to your house, and, if it's hot, dip your toes in a dried-up stream.

When I go there, I'm the town oddity—a single gal. This puzzles them, since they say I'm "well bred." The main reason I date, I confess, is for the old-fashioned, traditional one—to find a husband. The closest I came was when I was actually proposed to. I said yes. We decided we would get to know one another's families before making an announcement. In the meantime, my whatever-we-want-to-call-him was "keeping" the ring, but took it back to the store without telling me. When I imagine him, I imagine him "high-tailing it out of there" or "heading for the hills," as my family would say, in a dead run.

For my mother, landing a husband was easy. During her dating years, conservative folks, at least the young ones, simply went to one another's houses and weren't allowed to visit unless a relative was supervising. I think of her small

waist, her dark hair bouncing around her face, her dimples catching the attention of her first date, her high school math teacher, now my father. He was a
reputable man in town (in such a small town, people would know if he wasn't),
and, back then, the early sixties, sexual harassment wasn't an issue. Her parents
liked him, but they still made him leave their house by nine p.m. When the
clock struck, my Grandfather Beckham would say in a booming voice, "It's getting bedtime around here," and my Grandmother Gracie, embarrassed, would
rattle pots and pans in the kitchen so no one would hear.

Perhaps my problem with dating lies in the fact that I didn't get out on the
balcony soon enough. When a friend and I were on vacation years ago, a maid
came into our motel room, ready to fire up a vacuum cleaner, but my friend
said, "No. Wait. Let me get out on the balcony first. If you sweep around me,
I won't get married." A beautiful gal, still single, slim, with long, full, dark red
hair, her most recent date involved fixing a pork chop and mushroom dinner;
she went the whole evening unknowingly wearing a mushroom plastered to her
forehead.

Mushroom Sally and I, we're old pros at creative dating. This explains why
I'm out getting Farmer Bob's cows all in an uproar and why many Hoosier bachelors take up the sport of running.

* * * *

I've lived in Indiana for seven years, first in Bloomington, then in Evansville. The Crossroads of America used to literally be a place that I only drove
through with my parents during family vacations out west. It was like driving
across a table, and having gone from hills to flatness felt like standing at an
overlook surrounded by a rail and suddenly having the rail disappear. Back
home, unless you climb high, you rarely see a sunset, or the sliver of pink that
lines the horizon after the sun has slipped away. I've finally got used to the flatness, learned to love the fiery orange sunsets, then pale colors of evening. What
others complain of as being boring or lacking opportunity seems to me open
with possibility. I grew up in a place so small it was rare to see an airplane, so
whenever one flies over my house, I always watch, even though by now I should
take planes for granted.

I get annoyed with others' complaints about Evansville dating and some of
the tactics used to try and remedy the problem. One solution is speed dating,
organized by Rapid Rendezvous, a company founded by an Evansville resident.

Speed dating, featured on shows such as *The Oprah Winfrey Show*, was held at the Fox and the Hound tavern in November 2002. Likely victims—I mean candidates—apparently met other possible matches but only had three minutes to get to know one another. Michelle Brutlag of the *Evansville Courier and Press* describes the scene: "When the women nervously took their spots at the numbered tables, the men chose their first dates and, with the ring of a bell, they were off. The lights were low, the music turned down, and drinks close at hand." Of course, who would have time for drinking?

After each "rendezvous," each participant gave his date a score of "hit," "miss," or "second chance." The hitmen's (the men who marked "hit") e-mail addresses were sent to the "hits."

I imagine the ringing bell sounding like a cowbell and me starting a glass-shattering rendition of "Send in the Cows." Or maybe I would go the subtle route and just say "Moo." Maybe it's not the kind of bell. Second choice is the beep a microwave makes when the food is heated.

Then there's the time limit. Society is already too fast-paced, and many already move too quickly when dating, especially into the bedroom. In this short amount of time, the focus is once again on physical appearance and first impressions—the notion of love at first sight, a myth perpetuated by our overly romantic culture. We're taught that love comes and goes quickly. I for one want something with staying power besides the latest pantyhose.

Even though apparently the females decide if they want to e-mail a possible date back, I'm troubled that the men do the choosing and the scoring. As far as I'm concerned, one of the few things speed dating, this fancy fixer-upper, has going for it is word play.

* * * *

What options do southwestern Indiana professionals have for meeting people? In Evansville, there is a singles group and another group, the Museum Contemporaries, that organizes events such as wine tastings and Halloween and Christmas parties. The problem is, because these groups are small, so many people end up dating one another that they often end up feeling like the dating pool consists of a bunch of recyclables. You risk losing friends if you're dating someone a friend has dated.

Evansville nightspots don't often have the flavor we're looking for, although some of the names move us to go in, usually only once. Prime examples include the Duck Inn or Dogtown Tavern (we Hoosiers have an affection for animals), a dive in a river neighborhood; it closes early—8:30-9:00-on-a-weekday early.

Recently, bars such as The Jungle and The Deerhead hosted original music nights, where musicians who wrote their own music performed. Evansville does have an outstanding philharmonic orchestra. Unfortunately, it doesn't get many other good concerts because most of the arenas aren't large enough. We end up getting musicians that we thought surely must've kicked the bucket years ago.

What about those poor souls who are too slow for speed dating or too late for Dogtown? How do we find a date? We could try a coffee shop (there's a nice one in downtown Evansville, Penny Lane, which frequently displays artists' work), but, still, there are no guarantees, even when a suitor composes a heart-felt poem about dancing sperm and dedicates it to you.

I have a friend who only uses the referral system. Another suggests going to church or the supermarket. Many churches have singles study groups, but if you don't actually believe, you might show up wearing a beanie at the wrong place.

The supermarket? Yes, apparently said friend's tactic is to set himself adrift in the frozen food section armed with a handful of coupons. He swears it works. I have my doubts. People are shopping for other things. They're thinking, "Get in and out quick." My friend is naturally charming, but your run-of-the-mill Larry isn't going to be able to score after waltzing into the toilet paper aisle with a coupon for "squeezably-soft" Charmin.

Sure, the small-town ambience of Midwest life can cause one to invent creative date-hunting venues, but, if you're a target for being hit on, you've now got to watch your back at the grocery or gas station, even when paying at the pump. A guy named Bull, a friend of my hairdresser, who looked the way you'd expect a guy named Bull to look, hair cut close on the sides, long waves of it hanging in the back, hit on me at a beauty salon of all places. In the midst of spritzing and poofing, the topic of conversation turned to tattoos. Bull had one on his ankle. "What kind of tattoo do you have, Bull?" I asked. I was trying to pass the time.

"Why, it's a bull," he answered.

I guess he was happy that I struck up conversation because, when I was in a matchbox-sized room getting my eyebrows ripped off, clutching the armrests of my chair, he walked in and placed his hand on mine. "I don't want you to go through any pain."

Same principle as the grocery store. I'm a sucker for spontaneous romance as much as the next Juliet, but should some places be that multipurpose? Sometimes you just want to stick to getting your teeth drilled or buying your toilet cleaner and be done with it.

I once had someone hit on me at a restaurant by walking up and saying that his friend had noticed that I had an extra large foot and, by the way, what size shoe did I wear.

* * * *

I was on a date at Good Times, a restaurant in Bloomfield, west of Bloomington, where, during dinner, the spirited folks behind us got a worship service fired up. The singing was so loud my date and I couldn't hear one another. During the prayer, he stopped moving his fork, bowed his head, raised it, looked at me with one eye, said, "I don't know whether to eat or pray," and bowed his again. Apparently the dinners/church services were held every Tuesday, but we didn't read the sign out front.

During a first date with the same guy, at Bob Evans, we sat behind a couple "trying out" a baby. Said baby was a doll that behaved like a real baby, pooping, crying at unpredictable times. Our waitress kept burping the plastic wonder while my date and I smiled at one another and kept chewing. Chew, chew, chew. Our empty glasses loomed large. For a while, the baby slept on the floor in a carrier beside my date's feet. "I'm afraid I'll drop my coat on it," he said, his six-feet, four-inch frame peering down on it. "It? Do I call it an it?" Not the kind of situation that bodes well for trying to "ease" into a date with a commitment-phobic man. There was no first kiss, and my heart did not leap at this plastic baby whose eyes opened creepy slow as it raised its arms. "Friendly doll," I said. The mother gave me the stink eye. "I mean baby." Twenty-four at the time, I was not even close to thinking about motherhood.

Another date and I went to a Native American Days celebration at Angel Mounds. It's always a treat to watch Hoosiers, clad in heavy-metal-band T-shirts, jeans, and high tops, at a powwow, turning in circles, knees high in the air, searching for rhythm. He and I decided to explore a temple in an open field. There was a short brick wall around it, and the weeds were overgrown. As I rounded the edge of the temple, a kamikaze bee or wasp was going the opposite direction and flew into my face. He stung me twice right next to my eye, making the left side of my face swell to twice its size. I was put on medication. Maybe it was the spirits' way of saying the Hoosiers hadn't found rhythm and just needed to go on home.

Because Hoosier men love their cars, transportation is always an adventure in itself, especially when the guy likes to "build" his own vehicle. One date of mine built his own truck and was proud that he didn't have to have a key to turn it on. On a highway somewhere in Indiana, in winter, the truck stalled, and, in order for it to run, we had to keep the heat off. I rode with my fur-trimmed hood on, clutching it at my throat.

Then there was the date whose car's brakes fell out on the way to the movies. During the movie, he went back out to the road and picked them up, wrapped them in something, and put them under his arm. At a different time, the same date's car caught on fire right as we pulled up at a wedding.

* * * *

I understand some women's frustration with Hoosier men and vice versa. Consider this story: a man in Evansville—let's call him Affectionate Taco Guy—takes his date to McDonald's. On the way to the movies, Affectionate Taco Guy revs his engine, eases through the drive-thru at Taco Bell, orders two tacos, and doesn't ask his date if she wants anything. It gets better. Taco Guy raises his pant legs and stuffs the unopened tacos in his socks, one down the right one and one down the left. Date is silent and stares out the window, as if mesmerized by strip malls zooming by. Taco Guy drives on, not noticing her silence, that her jaw is clenched, or that she's hugging the door.

Later, the movie begins, and boy is his date glad. She suddenly feels safe, comforted by the sound of people chomping on popcorn. She doesn't mind that someone's elbow is on her armrest or that someone's foot is knocking against her seat. All the 1,000-calories-a-tub popcorn chomping sends Taco Guy's tummy to rumbling. Not to worry. He leans in toward his date, pulls a taco out of his sock. "Want one?"

* * * *

In spite of the horror stories, most of the few men I've loved have been Indiana boys. They don't stuff tacos in their socks, but it took me a while to give them the credit they deserve. At first, I resisted them, wondering if they were like the men back home. I grew up with a love for any kind of art—writing, painting, music—which many didn't have an interest in. I grew up learning classical piano and reading about places other than where I was from.

Partly in an effort to escape my roots, for a while I dated foreign men. There was Jarko, the Finn who wore socks with the toes in them, and the money-hungry, worried-about-his-own-image Swede, Klas, who said we should begin a date by asking one another questions. He stuck his foot out from under the table. "Do you like my shoes?" We didn't make it to Christmas. I had both looked forward to and dreaded hearing what jokes my relatives would make about his name. There was Tore ("Too-ra"), the Norwegian whose name I couldn't pronounce without first having to do a flamboyant mental rendition of "Toora Loora." There was Luis, the Spaniard who wore black driving gloves no matter the time of year and danced as fast as he drove his Porsche along the Ohio River. I couldn't keep up. There was the Parisian who lived under a roof of glass, watching stars all night long. He didn't keep pictures and claimed to not know his age.

The ones who won my poor, rejected heart were the ones who wanted to go on long drives across snow-covered fields in Indiana in the dead of winter and look at covered bridges or ones who wanted to picnic beside lakes, such as the storm-water engineer who spent much time during our walks looking down inlets. We would often go out during storms to study the unruly rise of water. They understood my connection with the land. The guys back home loved nature, too, but many of them thought the wild was only a place for men to drive into on four-wheelers, set up camp, load guns, and sharpen knives—not a place to be shared with a woman, unless she was frying up some good pork.

The Indiana men laugh a lot, are intelligent and cultured, are laid back but with a sense of adventure. We can go mountain biking at a place east of Bloomington called Gnaw Bone Camp, where we race down a hill called Hoot 'n Holler (really, it's not what you think).

The Indiana men bond with people around them, even strangers, whereas men back home can be too quiet and stoic. Once a date and I were hiking to a shelter at Audubon Park, across the river from Evansville, during the first big snow of winter. Inside the shelter, we happened upon a couple who had built a fire, so we sat across from them on a bench, enjoyed the warmth, and gave them half of our stromboli.

Another date and I went to a Christmas celebration at New Harmony, an extremely small, utopian community, with attractions such as a roofless church and a garden with tall, canopy-producing trees and a maze surrounding a lighted center fountain. We happened upon two little girls building a snowman. He asked them if the snowman needed eyes, pulled two wrapped peppermint candies from his pocket, and stuck them in the ball of snow.

This same man once fed people grapes on a hiking trail when they passed us. Some hesitated and looked at him like he was crazy. One huge guy who had a white beard popped one in his mouth without pausing, said, "Ho, ho, ho," like Santa, and walked on. The date also, after a race, saw a very short, ninety-year-old woman walk across the finish line, walked up to her, and put her on his shoulders. He had a way of making me feel I'd gotten two dates out of one.

* * * *

I wonder what my thirties will hold for me. Although my story is different than my mother's and I've been brave with dating, I know how hard it is to truly know someone. Background checks could be a good thing. I imagine sending each prospect through a machine similar to the kind at airports. His insides would light up with all the baggage to be weary of: Killed five people in 1981. Issues with mother. The thing with the dog.

You can see why speed dating scares me. I sympathize with the women, God help 'em, waiting for the bell to ring and for Joe New Person to saunter over to their table and try to catch his breath fast before those three minutes are up. However, the background check is not a good way to live, either. Each takes away the mystery. Thank God we've got plenty of that here in southern Indiana.

Doorways into the Depths

AS WE DREW UP to the brink of the old quarry, bullfrogs flopped into the water, a slimy brew mint green with duckweed, and a painted turtle cruised into hiding, its shell bright red around the edges as if colored by a child. A vine clinging to a log turned into a blacksnake and slithered away. It was a small hole, about the size of a three-car garage, five floors deep, and rank, fecund, a swarmy pit where life might start all over again on its evolutionary spiral. The season was late May, the ginger and jack-in-the-pulpit newly out, a dogwood growing on the narrow lip between the second and third floors was dropping a blizzard of petal-like bracts on the water. Presently the bullfrogs resumed their croaking. From the limb above the water a pewee whistled its name, over and over. A beggarly scrawking leaked steadily from a woodpecker hole in a dead tree, where a chick with a brown fluff ball for a head was begging fiercely for grub. My photographer friend, Jeff, and I had to raise our voices to make ourselves heard above the racket of spring.

We were hunting a place that would give us a feel for what the life of a quarry hand might have been like in the long-gone days. We found it here, at the Old State House Quarry on McCormick's Creek. The site is less than half a mile above where the creek empties into the White River. If you come by water and perch on a flat rock in the middle of the current, you can see why they chose to dig in this place. The bank is a solid bluff of limestone forty feet high, slightly undercut by the stream, like a smooth gray paunch. It is so unblemished that even the ferns and mosses find few places to curl their toes. The soil on top is thin, easily stripped. On the day I sat there balanced on a teetery rock in the middle of McCormick's Creek, admiring the bluff, a fine mist of pollen swirled in the air. Driven slantwise by the wind, it looked like gossamer filaments in the sunlight, as if the threads of the universe were showing.

Leaving the bluff in place to keep the creek out, the quarriers began their hole about twenty feet in from the bank. They started work in the fall of 1879, digging stone for the new Indiana capitol. (If you snoop around the Indiana Statehouse you will find a plaque listing all the political bigwigs who held office during the decade of construction; you will find memorials to presidents, generals, pioneers, a temperance leader, a poet, even Indians and coal miners, but you will not find a word anywhere about the men who dug or cut or laid up the stone for this twelve-acre building.) The working day was ten hours long, and the pay was fifteen cents an hour. For boys, who carried buckets of drinking water slung from yokes around their necks and gathered up tools and passed on hand signals, a day's wage was seventy-five cents. Men and boys, they had grown up on farms and took it for granted that by nightfall a body would be too weary even for swatting mosquitoes. Many of them had come to work in the quarries from scratch-dirt places where the earnings were poorer and the hours longer. When it rained, the pit filled up like a tub, and they sloshed about in water. On frosty mornings their hands stuck to the tools and stone. When the sun poured down they baked in their rock oven, cut off from breezes, the walls holding the heat.

At night they slept beside the quarry in cabins raised on piers, the few married men in private huts, the single men in a communal dormitory. The nearest towns were Spencer, by the dirt road, and Gosport, by the river, neither one close enough for walking after a day's work, neither one very much of a place when you got there. So in the evenings they sat in that malarial bottomland beside the creek telling stories, drinking, gambling, singing ballads, drinking, playing mouth organs and banjos, and drinking. They often pooled their money to buy whiskey in bulk, ordering it by the barrel. Whatever money they had left over they loved to bet on cards or dice, fistfights or races. If they had something to get rid of—an extra gun, a watch, a foot-broken pair of boots—they would wait for payday, sell chances, and then raffle it off.

When they finally did get to town on weekends, they found some dry-goods stores, a few churches, half a dozen clubs, and plenty of saloons. Often the stores belonged to the men who owned the quarries, so the workers, buying tobacco or socks, paid their wages right back to the bosses. The old-time quarrymen made little use of the churches. They had a reputation for godlessness, and lived up—or down—to it. For a while an eager minister from Bloomington lured them in fair numbers to his church, but he was soon turned out by his congregation, who objected to having all these rough customers in the pews. The quarriers saved their zeal for the fraternities, becoming Odd Fellows, Knights of Pythias, Red Men, Modern Woodsmen. (A limestone plaque on the Improved Order of Red Men Lodge in Spencer shows a peace pipe, a tomahawk, and the profile of an Indian who looks like a cross between a Roman gladiator and an Incan chieftain.) The saloons provided them with fresh settings for the familiar diversions of gambling and drinking and scrapping. Come Sunday night, back they went to their cabins beside the quarry.

The cabins, even though elevated on piers a yard or so above the creek bottom, must have flooded every spring. The spring of our visit, the high water marks on the sycamores were just above my head. Piebald sycamores, liking wet feet, were the only trees that would root in this boggy ground. They enjoyed the muck so well, in fact, that they often grew in clumps, like bundled stalks of celery, each trunk a yard thick at the base. When the quarriers lived here, before the creek bottom was lumbered over, some of the hollow granddaddy sycamores were roomy enough for stabling a horse or—in a pinch—a family. Cross sections of the solid ones, cantankerous and unsplittable, provided giant wheels for oxcarts. The upper limbs of the humbler trees we saw were laced together with grapevines. Meanwhile the flowers were putting on their May extravaganza: blue of waterleaf, pale rose of wild geranium, white of mint and false Solomon's seal, scarlet of columbine and fire pinks. Knee-tall reeds and horsetails, pulpy plants straight out of the Jurassic swamps, pushed up between the flowers. Had there been a brontosaurus in the neighborhood, it would have felt right at home. Old-timers call horsetail the scouring rush because its cell walls contain silica and a fistful of it makes a dandy pot-scrubber. The ancient ancestors of this spindly plant grew to a height of sixty or eighty feet. Sunk in the swamps three hundred million years ago and baked in the slow oven of the earth, they formed the coal that runs the generator that makes the electricity that powers the machine I'm writing on this very minute. Coming on the lowly horsetail reminded me of the pertinacity of plants. Here they grew, frail jointed reeds that were older than the creek, older than the whistling birds, far older than the two-legged mammals, nearly as old as the limestone.

High waters closed the State House Quarry after only two years. The blocks had to be hauled across the White River to the railroad, and floods kept taking out the bridge, so after a couple of wet springs the site was abandoned. Now all we could see of the settlement were the stone piers, watched over today by a pair of garter snakes, snazzy green with yellow racing stripes.

* * * *

Because it lay across the White River on the railroad side and because it yielded sixty feet of good stone, the quarry at Romona—the people around here pronounce it "Roll-moany"—was kept open for a century, from the 1860s until the 1960s. "What finally shut it down," according to a farmer we met there picking up stones in a field, "was these two men who owned it died and the widows got so old they didn't know Monday from Sunday. Then one of the widows died and the other went crazy. They had to put her away. And she wasn't hardly out the door before the relatives got to fighting over who owned the place, and the next thing you know the lawyers got into it, and now there it sits, a world of stone and nobody working it."

Somewhere in his fifties, filling his chocolate-colored T-shirt to more than capacity, the farmer was a glowering man who gave off an aura of bitterness. The field he was standing in had just been cleared, and the bulldozer he had cleared it with, still ticking from the effort, hulked there beside him. Stumps and brush and weather-gray boards were heaped along the edges, ready for burning. A wagon hitched behind a John Deere tractor was parked within throwing distance. Every now and again as we talked, the farmer picked up a fist-sized rock from the dirt and heaved it clattering into the wagon. We had stopped to ask him about Romona quarry, whose derricks we could see rising from behind a screen of trees at the back of his field. Would he mind if we went to have a look at it?

"Damn right, I'd mind. What the hell you want to see it for?" He squinted at us with eyes like disks punched from an iron skillet. "You want to break your legs? You want to break your neck? You want to get yourselves *killed?* God *damn* it all to hell. Every time I turn around, honey, there's somebody sneaking back there fishing or necking or hunting or just screwing around. Blame fool go in there and break his neck, and the insurance will ruin you. You ever buy insurance? It's sky high, honey, let me tell you."

From all of this I concluded that he owned the land.

"Naw, naw," he said. "This bunch out of Ohio owns it now. All they use is the gravel. You want to go look at it, you got to get their say-so."

"In Ohio?"

"Naw. They got an office in Spencer." He chucked a lump of stone at the wagon. Bang. Clatter. "I'm just clearing this field for them. Get it in corn, put it to use."

I looked at the weathered boards in the burn piles. "What was here before you cleared it?"

"Bunch of them shacks the quarry workers lived in. Little bitty things you couldn't swing a cat in. Rattraps."

Jeff and I exchanged a grimace. We had missed seeing the old cabins by a few hours. "Did you work in the quarry?"

"Hell, yes, I worked there. Twelve years, starting in 1948. I was just married, you know, and pissing vinegar for a job. A cousin told me to come out and he could get me on. Shoot, I told him, they ain't got any work out there that'll hold me. And don't you know, honey, inside a year I was right up at the top, and I stayed there till the quarry shut down."

Here I drew another false conclusion. "At the top? You were ledge foreman?"

"They didn't have sense enough to make me foreman. What I got to the top of was the derricks." It was his job every week to oil the gears on the hoist engines and the huge black wheels, wide as truck tires, on the stiff-leg derricks. He could oil the wheels on the boom from the ground, but the wheels on top of the mast he had to climb to, a hundred feet up a swaying steel tower. "You talk about *dangerous*. You get on top and the wind's blowing. Nothing to hold on with but one hand, and that's greasier than pig fat. Nobody else but me would do it. I saw an oiler fall from up there once. He screamed all the way down the derrick and six floors down into the quarry. When we picked him up he wasn't nothing but a sack of bones."

This led the farmer into a vehement recital of other quarry deaths. "Once this old foreman was standing between two blocks on the grout pile, honey, and the whole thing shifted, and his bottom half was squashed so thin you could just about see through it." A show of thickness, crusty palms half an inch apart. "We dug him out with the derrick and drove him up to the hospital in Greencastle, him moaning all the way. But he was deader than a hammer when we got there." Another time a drill-runner sat leaning against a tilted block to eat his lunch. "When it fell over, he never knew what hit him. Never drawed a breath or made a peep. Shoot, honey, I'm telling you a quarry's a damn dangerous place."

For half an hour he fumed on about men electrocuted when channelers cut through wires, men smashed by derrick hooks, men ground up in machinery, buried under mudslides, scalded in explosions, drowned in trenches, men whose hearts burst from lifting or hammering. "They never made a nickel off that hole after all them poor sons of bitches got killed. Even without the two widows taking it over and going crazy and all the lawyers fighting over it, the quarry was done for." He swore randomly, cramming his sentences full of angry words. Yet even while swearing and glaring at us with his skillet-hard eyes, he kept calling us "honey," the way my Mississippi kinfolks used to do.

I eased him onto the subject of corn, then soil, then fish, hoping he would relent and say we could go on ahead and have a look at the quarry. But when I asked him again, he snarled, "Hell, no. I won't have your blood on my head. First thing I know, honey, one of you'd break your damn leg and the other'd break your damn neck, and then there'd be hell to pay with the insurance."

So we left him there in his bulldozed field picking up rocks, which he flung at the wagon with the furious determination of a relief pitcher nursing a one-run lead in the bottom of the ninth.

After a half dozen phone calls, a cautious official at American Aggregates finally said yes, we could explore their quarry at Romona, if we promised not to sue. The day we drove back out there opened with a thundershower, and continued misty and cool. The farmer wasn't in his field. We parked down the road a piece, where the old railroad switch from the quarry joined the main line. The bulldozer had been at work here, too, ripping a muddy track through the woods for logging trucks to use, clearing an old house site. The house itself must have burned. A twisted ironing board and melted television cabinet lay inside the foundations on a bed of cinders.

The bulldozer had shoved to the back of the clearing a tiny shed, its joints awry. The roof was covered with black shingles, the walls with yellow asphalt siding meant to look like brick. Where the siding had peeled away, paintless boards showed through. They reminded me of the oak planks on a pigpen my father used to have. The shed in fact was about the right size for three prime hogs lying side by side. But the last occupants had been human, for inside I found a bottomless kettle, an oil heater, a burst shoe. I couldn't stand up in there, and neither could anyone else who's taller than about five feet. In the lone, glassless window a rag of lace tablecloth hung down for a curtain, sashaying in the breeze. Behind the shed was a one-holer privy, its door open. Around the fertile foundations grew clusters of white star of Bethlehem, nodding timothy grass gone to seed, and waist-high ferns.

"Do you think some of the quarriers lived here?" said Jeff.

We had no way of knowing for sure. Neither of us liked to think of *anybody* sleeping here, least of all a man who staggered home bone weary after ten hours of muscling stone.

We staggered to the quarry through the woods. I led the way. Trusting my sense of direction, Jeff labored along behind with the tripod and camera over his shoulder. By way of rutted logging tracks, ravines, bramble patches, and wet thickets, I did eventually guide us to the Romona pit, only to discover there two fishermen, fat as Buddhas, who told me we could have sauntered in along a broad cinder path. Jeff commented on my orienteering skills. I asked the fishermen about their luck. They'd caught only a single bluegill, but—Lord, Lord!—they'd seen bass as long as your leg, bass so big if you ever caught one you'd need a cart to haul it home, bass of mythical strength and cunning. We listened skeptically. Then we trekked down to one end of the huge pit and peered over the edge. And Lord, Lord! There were bass straight out of fairy tales, as long as a forearm if not a leg, their bodies dark shadows against the pale rubble, idling in the murky water like apprentice sharks.

The quarry itself was on a scale worthy of the fish. After a century of digging, men had left a trench broad and long enough to hold ocean liners. At its deepest, from ridgeline to the underwater bottom, the drop must have been a hundred and twenty feet. Only a serious swimmer could have made it from end to end, and would have had to navigate around peninsulas of cattails, where redwinged blackbirds were fighting for territory, and past archipelagos of tumbled blocks. In the great hole the reverberating voice of bullfrogs sounded like diesel trucks shifting gears. The stair-stepped walls, rising story after story, looked like the ruins of a Mayan temple.

Three derricks had been left in place at one end of the trench. Their supporting cables intersected overhead in a spider's web. A kingbird and a crested flycatcher hunted insects from the guy wires, flitting out for the kill and then perching again to survey the gulf of air. The steel masts bled rust onto the rocks below. In paint even brighter red than the rust from the derricks, somebody had scrawled the word LIFER here and there on the quarry walls. Everywhere the word appeared, it had been peppered with rifle fire. In some of the pockmarks the bullets were still visible, buried up to their midriffs in stone.

From the ledges, hundreds of yuccas thrust up the green swords of their leaves, and the red blossoms of columbine drooped like the falling sparks of Roman candles. On our way back down the cinder path to the car, we surprised a gray fox, which took off loping ahead of us at a dignified pace, tail and spine undulating like a dolphin cutting water. It was not the first or the last of the foxes we saw around the old quarries, but it was unusual because of its color— red foxes prefer stony ground, gray ones prefer brush and woods—and because it showed itself at midday. Usually we saw foxes at the edges of the day, early morning or dusk. They would lift their muzzles and prick up their ears when they caught a whiff of us, then give us a long, curious stare before trotting off with the smug air of aristocrats. Coyotes also make their lairs in the old grout piles, we were told, but they're even shrewder than foxes, and we never met with any. Back at the car, eating our cheese sandwiches and apples, we were visited by a ruby-throated hummingbird. It rested for a minute on a telephone wire, then zipped away, headed for a drink from the red fountains of the columbine.

* * * *

At midsummer, on the stone lips of abandoned quarries, columbine is replaced by the tough open field wildflowers: the luminous orange of butter-fly weed, the creamy bursts of multiflora rose and the white tracery of Queen Anne's lace, pink everlasting pea, purple joe-pye weed, red clover and bull this-tle, violet garden phlox, lavender vetch, blue chicory. They make quite a show in the dog days, a garden no one plants and no one weeds. The high summer sun also deepens the green of quarry water. On the topographical maps these wet holes appear like scars, as if the land had been ravaged by smallpox. Zoom-ing over at five hundred feet, jets from Grissom Air Force Base use the belt of quarries for navigation, flying up the seams of glinting scars. On foot you swel-ter across green fields and stare over the edge into green pools, field blurring into quarry. Algae bloom down there like brown clouds, confusing the issue. Sky and underearth meet on the shimmering surface.

Fish eggs ride into the water-filled quarries on the feet of ducks. Bluegill, crappie, bass. Swimmers ride there on bicycles and motorcycles, in pickups and convertibles. The last few hundred yards they'll walk, if the water is clear and deep enough. Afraid of stony silence, they come with radios. To domesticate the raw pits, they bring air mattresses, coolers of beer, footballs, crinkling sacks of groceries; they park their vehicles within easy reach, ready for a getaway, like cowboys afraid to lose sight of their horses. They'll do all they can to transform the quarries into backyard swimming pools.

Near Bloomington a rusty-bearded man named Rob Titlow has spent eight years loading mail trucks at night, studying law in the daytime, and on weekends turning one of the quarries on the land he rents into a perfect swimming hole. He picked out this cratered land from a helicopter, after surveying all the quarry country for a likely place. "I didn't grow up around limestone," he told us. "But when I finished with Vietnam and came here to school, I got to where I loved the overgrown grout piles and the wet holes and the rusty derricks sticking up against the sky."

He'd like to turn his two hundred acres into a wildlife refuge, if he could get together enough money to buy the land. "We have beaver, foxes, coyotes, quail, pheasant, and so many deer it makes my buddies at the post office cry just to think about it. But I don't allow any hunting here." Fifty of those two hundred acres have been quarried. "When the stone companies finished with a pit they'd dump it full of trash—cables and channeler rails and broken machinery—to discourage swimmers. I chose the prettiest hole and went diving in it and cleaned out every bit of junk. Truckloads and truckloads. Then I stocked it with bullhead minnows to get rid of the algae. They're like vacuum cleaners, and they won't nibble on you the way bluegill do. Now it's about as fine a place for swimming as you'll find. I try to keep everybody out except my friends."

Titlow's circle of friends must be large: on the day we visited, there were nine cars and two bicycles parked at the head of the path leading to his perfect swimming hole. All guests observed two unwritten rules: to leave one another in peace, and to wear no clothes. "The guys who work at the quarry that backs onto my property like to park up on the ridge and watch the women. I hate it, because the reason my women friends come out here is to get away from the whistlers and gawkers. But I can't really hassle those guys. If they got mad and dumped a barrel of oil in my quarry, the place would be ruined for swimming."

The ordinary wet holes, which no one has groomed for swimming, are lethal places. Almost every summer a few swimmers are hurt or killed. Diving from the ledges, a man cracks his skull on rubble hidden beneath the soupy surface. A girl paddles into the mouth of an underwater cave and never paddles out. Grabbing a wire, perhaps thinking to swing out over the water and play Jane of the jungle, a woman is electrocuted. A boy, while frogkicking along the bottom, gets caught in the submerged skeleton of a derrick. Owners post warnings. Newspapers run horror stories. But the swimmers return every summer with the stubbornness of migrating caribou. A cashier in a plumbing store told me that when she was in high school she and her friends once found a dead cow floating in their favorite hole, but they just pinched their noses and jumped in anyhow. Summer after summer the sheriff's men make raids, sometimes arresting the swimmers by dozens; but they do so with half a heart, because most of the sheriff's men, when boys, swam in these same treacherous pits.

* * * *

The old quarries are doorways, opening down into elemental depths. They seem to inspire elementary passions in people, or to attract people whose primal urges have already been roused. Within the space of a month, rambling on my own, I witnessed three scenes that have stayed with me.

A red pickup, so heavily loaded that its rear bumper was nearly scraping the ground, backed to the edge of a roadside quarry. Two women hopped out and peeled a tarp away from the bulging cargo, which appeared from where I sat to be a small household's worth of furniture. Judging by their angry conversation while untying the ropes and by their matching cheekbones, the women were mother and daughter. The older one barked orders, the younger one sullenly replied. The mother was about forty, husky, as quick on her feet as a boxer, hair rolled up in a brown beehive. The daughter was in her middle teens, skinny, languid, face shadowed, and hair hidden beneath a railroad engineer's cap. When the last rope was undone the mother seized a rocking chair and heaved it over the lip of the quarry.

"I'll teach that son of a bitch!" she yelled. She kept on yelling about a man whom she never named as she threw stools, lamps, tables, cardboard boxes stuffed with clothes, armload after armload over the side. The stuff landed with a sploosh or a muffled thud, depending on whether it hit water or stone. Every now and again the woman hollered at the girl to help, but the daughter hung back, hands stuffed in jeans, face tight.

"He can't treat me that way!" the mother shouted. Over went a small television, the drawers of a rickety dresser, a pair of chrome-armed kitchen chairs. "Get your hands out of your pockets and *help* me," she cried as she wrestled with a sofa. The daughter never stirred. The sofa tumbled over anyway, and after it a mattress, bedstead, rolled carpet, boots, and a Sears catalog.

Eventually the truck was empty. The mother had never ceased yelling at some absent and beastly man. The daughter had never budged from her sullen pose. I watched it all from thirty feet away, squatting in the sun beside my parked bicycle, and all the while neither woman took any notice of me. Then as she slammed the tailgate, the mother glared at me and hollered, "And you can go to hell!" I sat tight, mum, not wanting to join that other man's household goods down at the bottom of the quarry. The pickup peeled gravel when it left.

Another evening, and in another quarry, I was sitting on the steps of a caboose. When this pit was yielding up stone, the caboose had served as the foreman's office. Now it served me handsomely as a perch, from which I could study the darkness thickening among the limestone ledges. A shadowy figure broke the skyline and walked past me to the lip of the quarry. It was a man, rather stooped, and he carried something rolled up in his hand. I could make out nothing more definite in the darkness. There was the click and flare of a lighter. In a moment, whatever the man was grasping became a torch. He lifted it up near his eyes, giving me a glimpse of an old man's face, wrinkled as a dried apple, solemn and impassive. Was it a will? I wondered. A marriage license? Bundle of bills? Love letters? Poems? And why had he brought it here, instead of burning it in the fireplace at home, or in his driveway? When the flames were guttering down near his fist, he dropped the torch onto the stone. In a slow shuffle he circled the fire. Once, twice, three times. On each drowsy orbit his cratered face waxed and waned, moonlike, in the reflected light. It was a primordial dance, a banishing of some evil. Whatever the source of his dread, it required this stony place for its exorcism. After the last spark winked out, I heard his shuffling steps go by the caboose, almost near enough for me to reach out from my cloak of invisibility and touch him.

In the third and last of these little passion plays, I was planted like a seed in a waterworn cranny high in the wall of a quarry. Of course it was a womb that held me. But it was also an ancient seabed, a good place for sinking down into the depths of the mind. The day was hot, crazy hot. A red-tailed hawk circled in lazy loops overhead, waiting for anything with blood in it to show itself on the rock. An old wooden water tower, held together by rusting steel bands, leaked a constant stream onto the ground nearby. I was reflecting aimlessly on the hawk and water and stone when a van pulled up. On the side a desert sunset had been painted in Day-Glo colors. Three men clambered out, all in baseball caps advertising beer, each with a can of beer clamped in his fist, each a bit loose in the joints of the legs. One of them caught my eye in particular, for he was remarkably fat above the waist and scrawny below, like a keg balanced on a sawhorse, and to show off his physique he wore the sort of belly-length T-shirt favored by svelte tailbacks.

This one led the way to the quarry lip, just around the corner from the niche where I was planted. He jammed the beerless hand into his pocket and drew out a revolver. Bam bam bam. He fired down into the water—at no particular target, so far as I could tell from the scatter of splashes. His two buddies also tugged handguns from their pockets and began pumping lead into the green pool. The noise hammered around in the quarry like a maniac in a padded cell. Maybe they were aiming at the fish, which veered in silver bursts, scaly sides catching the light like a slant of wind-driven sleet.

The trio emptied their guns, reloaded, emptied them again, three times, and on the fourth round they began firing at the walls. They laughed, hearing the bullets zing and ricochet off the stone. I was not laughing. I had crawled so far back into my crevice that it would take a good lubrication of sweat to get me unstuck. They might have killed me by accident. But they might also, I was convinced, have killed me on purpose. It would have seemed more in keeping with their helter-skelter mayhem to have shot me than not to, and nobody could ever have known they did it. I kept well hidden. A quarry in a quarry. Except for their laughter, not a sound emerged from their throats. They spoke only in bullets.

By and by the shooting stopped, the van's motor started, the tires crunched away. I was a long time in coming forth.

Hoosier Hysteria

THERE USED TO BE giants abroad in the land.

There used to be heroes who walked among us.

There used to be legends, the deeds of whom were whispered about in awed tones.

Their names were Milan, South Bend Central, Muncie Central, Crispus Attucks, Gary Roosevelt, Kokomo High, Indianapolis Manual, Lebanon, Shelbyville, New Castle, Anderson, Michigan City High, Evansville Memorial, Batesville.

Their names were George McGinnis, Kent Benson, Steve Alford, Dick and Tom Van Arsdale, Oscar Robertson, John Coalman, Mike McCoy, Rick Mount, Bobby Plump, Ron Bonham, Jimmy Rayl, Glen Robinson.

Alas, like Poe's ebony-feathered subject of fiction, these personages are . . . Nevermore.

The Indiana High School Athletic Association killed 'em.

With a dastardly stroke of a pen—no doubt, a cheap ballpoint—Bob Gardner, he of the IHSAA, signed a document that destroyed the stage for the Greatest Show on Earth, no apologies whatsoever to the Barnum and Bailey folks, who, I guess, have reclaimed the title. Although, they probably don't want it. It's not a desirable title these days, not with the politically correct "Feel-Gooder" morons in charge.

Who held the title of the Greatest Show on Earth before the sluggards destroyed it?

Indiana. Most of the country knew it as—

Hoosier Hysteria.

Our high school hoops state championships. For those of you who think "March Madness" came from the national collegiate tournament, it originated with Indiana's single-class tournament. Alas, since the introduction of multi-class basketball, March Madness has been replaced with "March Enui."

Yes, you boys and girls who are too young to remember, gather 'round and let me lay something you may not be able to believe on you.

Indiana used to be a cool state.

It's the truth, hard as it is to believe. Ask an older person.

When I was a kid, my family moved back and forth between Indiana and Texas. In those days, Texas was renowned for high school football and oil wells, and the name "Hoosiers" was synonymous with high school hoops. Indiana also had Notre Dame football, and there was some kind of car race each year down in Indy.

Texas is still respected for its high school football. They've still got oil, but nobody's buying it much these days.

Indiana? Well, Notre Dame football went down for a few years, but it's on the way back. But then, they're not controlled by the state legislature, so they don't have to operate like Indiana University or Purdue University. They're actually free to pursue something called "excellence" in academics and sports. They're also in possession of a secret. The secret? Recruit players who played high school football in other states. Like Texas.

I'm not sure if they still have that Indy race thing, but then I didn't pay much attention to it even when it was something of a big deal, which I understand it was at one time.

And I guess they still play b-ball at some of the high schools, but personally, I wouldn't know.

The mediocrities got hold of it.

Created something called "multiclass basketball."

They also chased Bobby Knight from the state. Same types of characters, basically.

Now, we're known for . . .

I honestly don't know what Indiana's known for these days. I've asked around and nobody else does either. Maybe I'm asking the wrong folks, but I don't think so.

Maybe the lottery?

Or that soybean/cornfield thing.

That's something, I guess.

How'd this happen?

The losers gained control.

It's happening everywhere, so I shouldn't be surprised it happened here.

By "losers" I mean those mediocrities who either were too dumb, too lazy, or too uncoordinated to ever achieve anything by their own effort and talent. They couldn't do it themselves on the playing field, so they just changed the playing field. Put that current educational philosophy into play. You know, the one that says nobody should ever feel bad, that everybody should get to "win" no matter what their ability or effort. The "feel-good" concept. The concept that's leading us into a second-rate status as a nation.

If the "educators" in charge of the IHSAA had their way, every single high school in Indiana would end up at the end of the year with a "championship" (term used loosely). Knowing that to be impossible—at least for now—they did the next best thing. They divided the schools into classes.

And destroyed the only possible setting for greatness.

And, "great" is the only way possible to describe what used to take place in Indiana in March every year. Or, perhaps more appropriately—GREAT!!!—as the e-mailers and Tom Wolfe would put it.

There was nothing like Hoosier Hysteria in the entire universe, at least on this planet.

Here's something to illustrate how that grandeur that used to be has fallen. This was my experience, but I am not alone. Millions of Hoosiers did the same as I did, which was this: From the time I could read as a young boy, up until that infamous moment in 1997 when Gardner and his minions destroyed single-class basketball, each year when the tournament began, I would avidly pore over the sixty-four sectional winner results statewide. Even though I hadn't been to places like Shelbyville or Paoli or probably three-fourths of the proud towns who crowned sectional winners, I felt as if I was intimately familiar with them. It wasn't until I was in my twenties that I ever visited Kokomo, but I knew all about Kokomo long before I ever went there. Why? If you have to ask, you're either very young or from out of state, although many Americans not Hoosiers were aware of the skinny shotmaking machine that was Jimmy Rayl.

Jimmy Rayl was the personification of Kokomo, in my mind. A blue-collar worker who excelled on the court because of his work ethic, where he'd shoot five hundred baskets a night, in snow, in rain, in whatever. A work ethic like the citizens of the town itself I assumed exhibited, a great many of whom worked on the line at Delco on the graveyard shift.

I learned the geography and the personality of all the various towns and regions in Indiana from years of following the sixty-four sectional winners.

I knew that in East Chicago and Gary, in South Bend and Indianapolis, kids were big and tough and city-wise. I knew that in Evansville, there was something in the water that developed the "speed" gene more than most other places in the state.

I knew that Bremen grew hefty, wide-bodied German kids who wouldn't give an inch in the paint and played "football on a basketball court."

That Plymouth would have long, rangy forwards who could kill you with their deadly jump shots.

I knew Fort Wayne wouldn't go far most years, as they'd get killed by the tougher "street" kids from Muncie when they got to regional or South Bend if they got to semistate. Most years, they were just too soft, and that's how I saw the town. After eventually moving to and living in Fort Wayne, I see I was right.

I knew that at least one team from Terre Haute would have a superb point guard who understood the game better than most.

I knew a tiny town like Concord—one of those many Indiana burgs that dot the landscape and break up the monotony of the cornfields, a town where the "Entering" and "Leaving" town signs are on the same post—could every few years grow a player like Shawn Kemp and advance all the way to the title game.

I knew another village called Argos could put together a singular class of overachievers who could go far in the tournament. That it wasn't just Milan who made noise in the tourney, but many, many others over the years. Concord, Delta, Argos, Jeffersonville, Peru, Valparaiso, Franklin, Greenwood, Madison, Lebanon, Warsaw, Noblesville, Bloomington, DeKalb, French Lick; the list is historically long and rich.

I learned more about Indiana from following the sectionals each year than I ever learned in any Indiana history or geography class. I learned about a great state with a great bunch of people who came together every March to follow the greatest sports tournament in the world. No other state came close to matching the magic that was Hoosier Hysteria, and that was on the *sectional* level. By the time the Final Four rolled around, the populace was in a fever pitch. Each of the four regions rallied around "their" boys when it got down to the final games.

Winning even the lowest level of the tournament—sectional championship—was a thing people talked about for years and years. In schools that rarely won sectionals, the players on the teams that did (and even on the teams that only came close) were remembered for the rest of their lives by their fellow townspeople. You could walk into a barbershop in 1997, in say, tiny Tyner, Indiana, and a man would walk by and the barber, knowing you were a stranger, would point to him and say, "That's Rick Skiles. He played on one of the last teams before we were consolidated with Walkerton to form John Glenn High School and some went to Plymouth in the reorganization of the district. He was one of the best players to ever come out of here. If they hadn't consolidated and closed down the school here, his son Scott might have gone here instead of to Plymouth, and we might have won state." He might then go on to tell you that Scott Skiles was named an all-state player at Plymouth, went on to an All-America career at Michigan State University and then on to the NBA where he played (and still holds the single-game assists record), and then, after retiring, coached the Phoenix Suns. Today, he coaches the Chicago Bulls. A kid from a family that lived on the family farm for decades. Not the kid the IHSAA wants you to think is "denied" a chance for a state championship, from a South Bend Central or Indianapolis Manual.

That barber wouldn't have to tell me all this, as I played on the same team with Scott's dad Rick. Not anywhere close to his league, however, father or son.

The thing is, Hoosier Hysteria united citizens in every town and burg in Indiana like nothing else ever has. That's all destroyed now. That famous picture of a long line of cars leaving a small Indiana town and the caption underneath, saying, eloquently, "Last person out of town turn off the lights," can no longer fit the reality that multiclass basketball has brought us to. Sectionals used to be a *huge* deal in every single community in the state. Regionals were *enormous*. There isn't a word that sufficiently describes the impact of the semistate level, and someone will have to invent a term that can adequately describe the fervor for the Final Four. Oh, yeah—actually, they did have a term that said it *perfectly.*

Hoosier Hysteria.

No more. Not these days. Nowadays, nobody even goes to the state title games. Not much "hysteria" going on there. The old sectional at Anderson drew more fans than they do for the final game in any of the four classes these days. Heck, the Christmas Holiday Tournament drew more! Cameramen filming "title" games these days have to be really inventive to make it appear someone's actually in attendance. They don't dare aim their cameras much above the fourth row, as all the viewer would witness would be empty seats.

Nobody cares. Not even the schools and towns appearing in the "championship" games. The average Hoosier has more common sense than the folks in the

IHSAA. They know that only when a thing is achieved against great odds and against a formidable opponent does it have much value.

The value of our state tournament isn't worth much these days.

It is those feats performed by valiant warriors against daunting obstacles that define a people and even a culture. It used to be that when a person from Indiana was on vacation in say, Ketcham, Idaho, and a local asked him where he or she was from and they told him, the automatic response would most likely be, "Indiana, huh? The basketball state!"

Today?

"So, how many acres do you farm?"

And lest the uninformed reader think this situation applied only to the boys' version of b-ball, let me assure you that the first girls' tournaments elicited the same kind of passion from the fans when it was still a single-class tourney. I know this firsthand, as I was working in Warsaw when Judy Warren led her team to the very first Indiana state championship for high school girls.

I guarantee you Warsaw isn't Indianapolis or South Bend or Michigan City. It's a small town of about 15,000 folks. The "Milan" of Indiana girls' basketball.

Let me tell you a personal story about Judy Warren and that Warsaw team.

Some backstory. When I was a kid, I was like most boys in that I was sports-crazy. I lived in a Walter Mitty world, like most boys probably do, in that when I would listen to a game on the radio or see one on TV, I'd "become" that person in my mind. I can still remember "being" Oscar Roberson and Bob Cousy or Willie Mays. Immediately after the game I'd been listening to was over, I'd head outside with my basketball or glove in hand and go try to imitate the moves I'd just seen or heard described.

Sports were a huge part of my life. It just never dawned on me that girls were denied what I took for granted. Oh, sure; they had a thing called "GAA Basketball," a game played at half-court with six players (poor, little, weak things couldn't run full-court was the wisdom), and some bigger schools might have a girls' softball or volleyball team, but that was about it.

Judy Warren and her teammates revealed to me what girls had been missing from their lives. They gave me a lesson in inequality between the sexes that all the articles and speeches by the women's movement had never been able to.

At the time, I had just moved up from New Orleans and opened a hairstyling salon in Warsaw. We were living in Pierceton, a few miles away. On the day of the title game, I lay on my couch and watched Warsaw scrap and battle and emerge victorious.

A thrilling game.

What was even more thrilling was what happened next. Just as I switched off the set, something outside my window caught my eye.

Four young girls, around the age of twelve, came walking by. Dribbling a basketball and passing it around among themselves.

All of a sudden, I realized what they were doing. They were "being" Judy Warren.

Just as I'd "been" Oscar Robertson.

It hit me like a sledgehammer. All these years, girls had been denied the heroes I took for granted. They'd been denied the opportunity to be heroes themselves.

Just as we've taken that opportunity away from every high school basketball player in Indiana—boys *and* girls—with the IHSAA's insidious act in 1997.

The passion has been utterly destroyed. Never again will we see entire communities rallying behind "their" teams as in the past. Never again will we be able to drive down the streets of a Concord or Tyner or Lebanon or Muncie or Greenfield and see every single window in town—businesses and residences and cars—adorned with signs saying, "Go, Big Red." Never again can one enter a bar or a barber or beauty shop or diner and just about everyone in the place is talking about one subject—the merits of their local high school b-ball team.

Never again will we have to post a reminder for the last person in town to "turn out the lights" as the entire populace leaves for the sectionals.

Most everybody has stayed home to watch a Seinfeld rerun.

The story of mankind is writ via the lives of heroes.

And athletic endeavors have historically provided a larger-than-life milieu for heroic exploits.

Do you suppose they're going to make another movie like *Hoosiers* about Westview High winning the Class 2A State Championship in 1999? First, they'd have to find more than three people outside that community (and whoever they beat, which is an even more obscure factoid) who even knew they'd won.

Not bloody likely.

If such a movie were to get made, it wouldn't be Clint Eastwood or Gene Hackman who'd play the lead.

Think Alan Alda in one of his weenie, "sensitive" roles.

One of the architects of the IHSAA decision to institute class basketball, Bremen High athletic director Frank DeSantis, said, "It's awful nice coming back from Indianapolis with a big trophy in your hands." That's partially right.

For tiny Milan High School in 1954 it was. They actually played someone. David beat Goliath. The stuff of heroes. If DeSantis's Bremen H. S. hoopsters came back with one of those "big trophies?" Even from the players involved, one might easily get the same response Bobby Plump, the hero of Milan's heroic team, got from a kid from small-school Speedway High, who won the Class 2A championship last year. The boy came up to Plump and held out his championship ring and said, "I got one, too." Plump congratulated him, saying, "That's wonderful." The boy replied, "Well, it isn't so wonderful. I'd rather have played on an old sectional champ than won a state title."

This young man understood better than the IHSAA adults that merely "winning" something doesn't mean a thing unless you've won it against a formidable opponent.

The insanity continues. Now, they're trying to abolish dodgeball in gym classes.

They've taken away the only thing Indiana used to be considered great at.

Unless you count that soybean/corn thing.

There used to be giants that walked the earth in Hoosierland.

These days, it's midgets that mince . . . what the heck. You get it.

Welcome Home

"Home is the place where, when you have to go there, they have to take you in."

Robert Frost

How I Tried to Become a Hoosier

i.

"Birds do it, bees do it. Even educated fleas do it. Let's do it, let's fall in love."
Cole Porter, born Peru, Indiana

I BELIEVE I AM entranced by Indiana, birds, and bees. In my first months here, many of my colleagues at the university, themselves expatriates from the coasts, assume I must be suffering "coastal withdrawal" and rush to offer aid and succor, including tips for surviving deprivation in the hinterlands. They refer me to the local overpriced sushi bar and inform me there is no decent shopping until you get to Chicago, an easy four-and-a-half-hour drive if you put the pedal to the metal. Initiating the mutual dislocation patter of landlocked exiles, they invite me to launch into a litany of complaints about my new hometown.

I disappoint them. Sure, I concede, I miss the ocean, the red beacon winking off Alcatraz, the distant moody groans of foghorns, the fog spilling over Twin Peaks and slowly devouring the city, and the smell of salt air, or those unexpected splendid views of the city when you round a corner or top a hill on a crystal blue sky day and see it all laid out below you in sparkling symmetry. Yes, I miss the plethora of Asian, African, and Mediterranean restaurants where you can eat well and cheaply and where being a vegetarian does not draw looks of bafflement and the helpful suggestion to "just pick out the pork." And I yearn for the art theaters I once haunted, where I watched obscure documentaries and films from all over the world, often made on minuscule budgets with grainy stock by persecuted Third World directors in grave danger of retaliation from oppressive regimes supported by the United States. A far cry from the sophomoric offerings of *Big Mama's House* and *Toy Story 2* at our local theater monopolized by a corporation I refer to as "the Brothers K." And, sure, I miss the assortment of characters that people large urban areas, like the now-deceased Tom the Puppet Man or Merry Prankster Wavy Gravy, or one of my favorite flaneurs in his Catholic girl's plaid skirt and knee socks, loafers, and wig who one day went from perusing the lingerie display in a Lower Haight boutique window to leaping frantically into a Yellow Cab, or the small, shaved-head man in an institutional gray jumpsuit who roamed the Mission wearing a sandwich board covered with hand-drawn interdictions, including the final line at the bottom in minuscule print: "If you read this sign, I'll kill you."

Of course Bloomington is not San Francisco, but then San Francisco isn't either any more. The rise and fall of the dot-commers undid what remained of the middle class, and there is a huge gulf between rich and poor. In the Upper Filmore, the woman with the Coach bag strides in Gucci shoes past the homeless man pushing his shopping cart full of recyclable cardboard he's collected. No, it's not a heavy-handed scene from a movie; it really happens, every day, every week, with such regularity that it's no longer remarkable or even ironic. Sitting at the Elite Café's oyster bar drinking cosmopolitans at ten bucks a pop, you refuse without remorse to buy a rose from a little Guatemalan girl in tattered clothes and you have learned to ignore that moment when the maître d' shoos away the junkie couple standing in the doorway asking for leftovers. City traffic congestion makes driving an unpredictable adventure, even if you're just off to Rainbow Grocery for a little lemongrass or galangal root. There's no such thing as a fifteen-minute errand any more in the city. We used to joke that if you spotted an empty parking place in San Francisco, you should grab it, even if it's nowhere near where you want to go. In Bloomington, parking isn't always easy, but at least it's possible.

ii.

Some say the poet James Whitcomb Riley captured the spirit and vernacular of his fellow Hoosiers. I just always thought he was a very bad poet, with his maudlin moralizing and sappy sentiments. As a child, listening to his poem-with-a-moral, "Little Orphant Annie," read aloud (with its relentless refrain to warn children to behave: "the goblins will get ya if ya don't watch out!"), I had a sneaking suspicion even then it was terrible stuff. So it wasn't until I got to Indiana that I discovered he is still revered, at least according to various local historical societies, for representing the rhythms and expressions of Hoosier speech. So it is that I try to return to him with a less jaundiced ear.

But what do you do with lines like this?

One time, when we'z at Aunty's house—
'Way in the country!—where
They's ist but woods—an' pigs, an' cows—
An' all's outdoors an' air!—
An' orchurd-swing; an' churry-trees—
An' churries in 'em!—Yes, an' these—
Here redhead birds steals all they please,
An' tetch 'em ef you dare!—
W'y, wunst, one time, when we wuz there,
We et out on the porch!

Churry trees? Not possible, I think. Standing in my front yard in Blooming-ton, Indiana, on a sweltering summer day, baffled by the proliferation of mid-western flora, lush as a jungle, I glimpse my elderly Hoosier neighbor heading my way to introduce herself. The California license plates on the three vehicles of our aging fleet parked out front have been attracting neighborhood curiosity all week, and, in passing, my neighbor quickly sizes up our 1978 orange van with the rainbow sticker on the rear window, as well as the 1968 GMC pickup full of my husband's "treasures" and my indestructible 1981 Toyota Tercel. Politely overlooking the tangled mess in the yard, she welcomes me to Bloomington, observing that next spring I'll have "some of the prettiest pineys in this yard."

I'm not sure what pineys are, but am reluctant to start off our acquaintance-ship with a display of ignorance. I pore over the index in my Rodale's gardening guide and, finding nothing under that listing, then resort to my imagination: something along the lines of small pine trees or little spiky bushes, I think. Some exotic native plant. Maybe something like a churry tree.

As it happens, the following spring, my eyes peeled for pineys, I finally make the connection to the explosion of peonies, which long about April crowd the length of the tumble-down fence in startling reds, pinks, and whites, emitting an obscenely sweet scent from their big faces.

Later, since my neighbor loves the flowers so much, I offer to bring over transplants of the "peonies." She looks a little puzzled, hesitates, then says sweetly, "Well, okay, I guess so." Only when I arrive moments later with a wheel-barrow of peonies does her expression change to visible relief. My pineys now bloom in her yard too.

This isn't the only example of my mispronunciations. I say "motorcycle" instead of "motor-sickle" and "de-LUX'" instead of "DE-lux." I am still working on mastering "I might can do." On second thought, where is James Whitcomb Riley when I need him?

iii.

Most of the undergraduates and townspeople I know are born and bred Indi-ana natives, heirs of the requisite legacy of Indiana ancestry for which there is no substitute. In California, just about anyone can lay claim to being a Golden Stater, even those who arrived the week before clutching green cards, and the natives don't object. But only those deserving can lay claim to Hoosierdom, the threshold for which is set high and perhaps requires, in addition to ancestry, that one's psyche and form have been carved from the rolling landscape.

When asked where I am from, I am presented with a problem. Do you mean where I was conceived? Rome. Where I was born? That would be Switzerland, but I am neither Swiss nor "of there." Where I "grew up"? I could name sev-eral university towns and as many states. I've been a Wolverine, briefly a Prairie Stater and even more briefly an Old Line Stater, and then more long-term a Buckeye. My one remaining connection to Ohio now is purely ancestral, and my only reason for returning to Oberlin once a year is to visit my parents, who have lived in the same house for almost four decades. If I named the place I lived the longest and where I actually set down roots, it would be the San Fran-cisco Bay Area: Berkeley, North Oakland, and the city. In some ways, the Bay Area is the place where I really "grew up," the place I most feel "from." But now when asked, I name the place where I spend nine months out of each year, "Bloomington, Indiana."

"Bloomington!" responds the asker, with that gleam of recognition reserved for scandal. "So what do you think of Bobby Knight?"

What do I think? I ask myself. There is only one way to think about Bobby Knight, as far as I'm concerned. His voice plays briefly in my head.

"Effort? EFFORT!? What the fuck is that!? These guys are going to be fighting a war! They're going to be second lieutenants with their fucking lives at stake! If all they give is effort, you might as well get the body bags ready NOW! What the hell are you talking about, effort! We go for victory here."

By this man my seven years in Bloomington have been so defined or, perhaps, I should say, reduced. His name still functions metonymically for Bloomington. No matter where I travel, the mention of Bloomington is sure to elicit questions about Bobby Knight. The truth is that he is not a Hoosier at all. He was born a Buckeye, and now, thankfully, belongs to the Lone Star State.

iv.

The truth is I like Bloomington. Even my first introduction to the town, via the hour-long early February-bleakest-time-of-the-year drive from the Indianapolis airport down Highway 37 when I flew in for my campus interview, didn't daunt me. There were apologies all around for the weather, the gray skies, the starkness of the leafless trees, the icy chill of the wind that whipped at my too-thin coat. Did I yearn for California then? Only vaguely. I found Indiana exotic. Do I yearn for California now?

> Georgia, sweet Georgia, no peace I find
> Just an old sweet song
> Keeps Georgia on my mind

Hoagy Carmichael was born in Bloomington, Indiana, and he composed some of my favorite songs. Other famous Hoosiers I admire include Eugene Debs, Theodore Dreiser, Jimmy Hoffa, Forrest Whittaker, Michael Jackson (yes, I said it), Gene Stratton-Porter, David Letterman, and Johnny Appleseed. Though Madam C. J. Walker wasn't technically a Hoosier, she did set up her cosmetic business in Indianapolis and became the first black woman millionaire.

Bloomington is a mostly pleasant town, breathtaking in the spring and fall, sort of Norman Rockwell-ish in its traditions, still affordable, and, as the song says, "the livin' is easy." We arrived in our twenty-four-foot moving van in the tropical steamy jungle green of late June. In the evenings we opted for alley routes meandering towards downtown through the firefly-lit night, mesmerized by the hypnotic sounds and lush admixtures of jasmine and wisteria wafting over the fences. Our destination was the Irish Lion for fish and chips and beer. Never before have I been a beer drinker, but when in Rome. . . . Over time I have developed an appreciation for microbreweries, organic Sonoma County pinot noirs be damned.

My husband Steve, a rare breed known as "bona fide Californian" and very much "of" the West Coast (the mountains, the deserts, and the ocean), was fascinated with the hardwood forests, as well as the four distinct seasons. During our first year he was given to rushing out to stand in the middle of booming thunderstorms, for a glimpse of a passing tornado.

Eager to fit in, we order up the local newspaper, the *Herald Times*, pore through the letters to the editor and articles on local news, and proudly purchase flannel pajamas for winter, a Sears power lawn mower for summer, and a leaf rake for fall. Steve trades scuba diving for spelunking. I know, though, no matter how long I live here, I will never learn to "clog," and bluegrass—well, it's never been my thing.

Unlike San Francisco, it is way too easy to be considered eccentric in Bloomington. Often here I feel like one of the dandelions in my front yard, not interesting enough to be remarked on, just not particularly desirable.

The town is very family focused, and for the single or the childless, adult activities beyond the campus can be limited unless one is drawn to events like the Over-40's Singles Club sharing a buffet at the MCL Cafeteria in the mall or the Tuba Santas playing old Christmas chestnuts in the City Hall during the holidays. So it is music to my ears one day to hear a radio host from Indy railing against Bloomington as "that cesspool of liberalism," and I hear that Amy Goodman is coming to town.

"Wonder how long we have to live here," Steve muses, "before we're considered Hoosiers." A long time, I think. One of the first questions out of locals' mouths is, "You folks aren't from around here, are you?" It's not a hostile question; it's an observation. Who are we trying to kid? As Hoagy said,

> Some sweet day when blossoms fall
> And all the world's a song
> I'll go back to Georgia
> 'Cause that's where I belong

v.

The university, a beautiful imposing sprawl of limestone buildings and woods, plunked right down in the middle of town, exists *in spite* of the town, and both university and town, I think, suffer for it. Some local friends have mentioned they don't always feel comfortable going up to the campus for events, and some university friends have expressed either disdain for or ignorance of local events. One of my colleagues informed me haughtily one day after I'd used the word "Hoosier" to refer to a friend of mine born and raised in Indiana that Hoosier was derogatory, and I should avoid offending people by using it. Then why, I asked, do we have Hoosier Motors, Hoosier Liquors, Hoosier this and Hoosier that? She looked nonplussed. She hadn't noticed. When my novel came out, the local bookstore placed me in the "local author" section. For a moment I thought I'd arrived. I was a Hoosier. But I'm not, and it's not only because I wasn't born here. I have Hoosier friends who visibly blanched when they found out who my employer was—the university. This is pretty much a one-company town, and every year when the paper publishes the salaries of the top twenty-five folks at the university, I cringe. I explain to my piney neighbor that I don't make anything approaching those figures. She looks at me dubiously. I point to my house and my secondhand car. "Trust me," I say, "if I made money like that. . . ." But what am I implying?

University folks can be easily identified by not only their clothing and mannerisms and speech, but by the restaurants where they eat, like Little Tibet and Samira's, which serves Afghani food, and both of which offer vegetarian options. Locals go for meat and potatoes at Wee Willie's, Little Zagreb, or Ladyman's Café, or the all-you-can-eat platter at the Red Lobster. University folks seek out smoke-free, chi-chi venues like the Scholar's Inn for over-priced martinis and pita points with assorted Spanish cheeses and red pepper tapinade. Local folks fill up the smoky Office Lounge and drink beer and eat chips. The jockier university students in their IU logo wear hang out at sports bars near campus like Nick's and Kilroy's. Local teens cruise Kirkwood and College on the weekends in their tricked-out cars. We inhabit the same town, but we live in different places.

vi.

In my undergraduate classrooms I am initially stunned to look out over a sea of mostly white faces (this is very different in my graduate classes), unable to distinguish among my students. But it is from them that I begin to draw a clearer picture of my new state, not found in guidebooks. How else would I have ever known about such favorite pastimes as cow tipping or paintball? "You mean you don't know about tractor pulls?" one of my undergrad girls teased me. "And you mean you thought California had it all!"

Bloomington, I discover, despite its relative position in the state of Indiana as an oasis of enlightenment, is ultimately conventional, the physical manifestation of which is most readily apparent in the rows of fraternities and sororities dotting the campus and the Birthright and abstinence billboards on the edge of town. Unlike Berkeley, where Sproul Plaza literally teems with debates between the young socialists and born-again Christians at their respective tables, or where an itinerant, Bible-thumping preacher rails to a racially-mixed crowd of back-talking students that they are all doomed to hell, the Sample Gates on the west side of campus seem to usher in a staid quiet. Here, the closest we get to information tables are those manned by carefully coiffed promoters of Visa and Mastercard offering free bottles of Coke to students who fill out credit card applications. Students don't gather in the same way here, but instead move unobtrusively from one building to the next.

On campus I hear the familiar strains of Spanish, Chinese, Hindi, Italian, French, Yiddish, and Arabic being spoken. Just recently at my local health food store I noticed the sign advertising phone cards to Mexico ("tarjetas prepagadas"). According to the 2000 census, blacks make up only 4.24 percent of the population here, Asians 5.26 percent, and Hispanics 2.4 percent.

In Bloomington, after Benjamin Smith makes his murderous racist rampage through the streets, resulting in the brutal shooting of a Korean student outside a church about three short blocks from my house, signs pop up on lawns around town, announcing *Bloomington United Against Hate*. A worthy sentiment, I think, but in a town with so few people of color, Bloomington has never directly had to confront race, other than as an abstraction. Easy to talk about diversity and tolerance, two words I have come to despise, when one's own life is relatively untouched.

vii.

My favorite place to walk is the forest trail at Lake Griffy, just outside Bloomington. Both locals and university folks wander there. I never tire of the place, which is transformed by the changing seasons and the various angles of light at different hours of the day. No matter how many times I hike the trail, I discover new things, including snakes, toads, squirrels, plants, and deer, or the three baby raccoons who surprised me one day by popping out from behind a tree where they'd been hiding. I came to Indiana expecting to find the Limberlost Swamp, rendered so compellingly through Gene Stratton-Porter's famous novel, only to find out it had been drained in 1913. When I look at the encroaching "mallification" of Bloomington, the gradual disappearance of farmhouses, and the mushrooming of new subdivisions, I keep thinking that life in Indiana should somehow be more wholesome, more homespun.

Our neighbors' yards are made green through chemical treatments that arrive in large trucks. After the spraying is over, small warning flags are posted to prevent anyone from walking across these enticing, but toxic, verdant expanses, not unlike the green-iced cake Captain Cook used to tempt the Lost Boys.

Our lawn, such as it is, has been left undefiled, and in spring and summer is home to a field of dandelions and violets and clover. It is likely considered the blight of our neighborhood (my piney neighbor has offered me helpful suggestions for correcting the problem), but then I count on our being from California to explain the neglect. After all, we fit the cliché: we're vegetarians, contribute to the Green party, plant an organic garden in the summer, and oppose the war—it seems fitting that our yard grows wild. This is not recalcitrance on our part: the weeds, many of which grow to three or four feet, charm us. Red buds and roses of Sharon spring up wherever they choose. Shortly after our arrival, we received a stern written warning from the city informing us that if we didn't do something about the weeds ballooning near the street, we would be cited.

There are two giant silver maples in our yard, one in the back, one out front. They are imposing trees and in the summer shade the yard. During both winter and summer storms, they drop huge branches. It is only after we've been here a while that we are told silver maples are "junk trees," that they were planted because they grow fast, but die young. This description makes me think of James Dean, another famous Hoosier, whose life ended in a car accident at age twenty-four. He once said, "Dream as if you'll live forever; live as if you'll die tomorrow."

viii.

Our house is a small rundown fifty-year-old bungalow (what I call our "grandma house") in an older neighborhood near campus, with a mixture of locals and university folks. It is the sort of house that might be easily advertised as a "handyman's dream." We live at the intersection of two streets, one busy, one quiet. The busy street is an artery to the mall several blocks away, and the traffic patterns can, at times, comfortingly imitate the rhythms of an urban area. It is a favorite route of dog walkers and the occasional child on a bicycle, with helmet, and watchful parent in tow. Though the university is just a half mile away, I bask in the illusion of anonymity even when I'm out mowing the front lawn in cutoffs and a man's undershirt. In my yard there is an invisible fence, and I'm "off-limits" to the world.

There is something very charming to living in a neighborhood in a small, midwestern town. For one thing, everyone says hello as they pass. My neighbors stop to talk, something that rarely happened in San Francisco. John and I trade cat sitting, Betty and I trade daylily bulbs and gardening tips, Roger trades hiking suggestions, and all of us trade small talk on warm spring or summer days when we're outside engaged in what appears to be that favorite (and necessary) midwestern pastime: yard work. Sometimes I sit on my front porch just to see who walks or drives by. Here I yearn for connections I only imagined I had in California.

ix.

Wherever I've lived, I have always had a close rapport with my mailmen (with one exception, they have all been men), and Bloomington is no exception. My life revolves around the mail, partly because I used to travel a great deal and needed to arrange for my mail to be held or forwarded. In Berkeley, my mailman was a gentle stoner I'll call Art, but on whom little was lost, and who took it upon himself, perhaps as a duty, to inspect closely each piece he delivered. He shamelessly read postcards I received from my brother on the East Coast, with whom I played postal chess, and often offered me strategic suggestions. Or he'd mention casually the day after delivering a letter postmarked from overseas, "So I see you're going to be traveling again." One day, when I ran into him on the sidewalk below my apartment, he paused to observe that he was getting a real kick out of the fact that Alyce Miller was living next door to a summer subletter named Helen Deutsch. "Bet old Jung and Freud are chortling in their graves," he laughed. Art, it turned out, eventually went into rehab, and the last time I ran into him was at a friend's party in the city where we danced to Aretha in celebration of his recovery.

My first Bloomington mailman is a young guy I'll call Bert. Bert, like Art, is a seeker and a thinker. He always takes a good deal of time getting from house to house because he is of a reflective nature and takes in the world slowly and fully. One day after delivering our current issues of *The Nation* and *The Progressive*, he remarks he might be interested in taking a look at one of the cover articles on U.S. imperialism in Guatemala, if we don't mind, and of course only after we'd read it. Next time, it is obvious Bert has already helped himself. "Really good article in this issue on the Middle East crisis," he says, handing me my magazines at the door. "I didn't know you could get information like this." He mentions he's Lutheran and at church they've been talking about some of these issues. "I'll recommend this to my pastor," he says.

In addition to his curiosity about the world at large, Bert proves to be a storehouse of neighborhood information. He knows who's lived where and for how long, where they go in the summer, and so on. When I present him with forwarding mail cards for my summers in California, he smiles and asks me what I plan to do out there. Somehow I know he'll keep an eye on things. He assures me that in the event there's a substitute mail person, he will be sure to check the mailbox to make sure nothing's been left by mistake.

It becomes a ritual each March that Bert pauses in front of our magnolia, tips back his mailman's cap, and predicts, "Well, this year it may get through the late frost. This tree has only bloomed three times since 1989." The magnolia, it turns out, comes with a history, which Bert explains. It had been planted by mistake by the previous owners of the house (who were also the only other owners), a family named Peak, whose talents lay in yard work, not in house maintenance. Mr. Peak had assumed he was planting a small magnolia, but it turns out to be a large variety, so large in fact, that it dominates the front yard. After it grew to its full size, he apparently referred to it as "that sonofabitchmagnolia." Of the seven years we've lived here, the magnolia has managed to survive late frosts about half the time. When it blooms, it is indeed magnificent, filling up the front yard with its oversized pink blossoms the size of large teacups. I look at the magnolia and feel a part of its lore. It's a romantic notion, and one of those occasional gestures I make at belonging to this place. There is history here, I tell myself, but it is, of course, not really mine. When Bert changes routes, I feel a deep sense of loss. Bert was exactly what any displaced Californian would want from her Hoosier mailman.

x.

When I first imagined Indiana, I pictured men in white sheets burning crosses and stringing people up. Indiana has a heavy Klan history. When I would drive out in the country here, along rural roads, the sight of Confederate flags flying from people's homes gave me the chills and obscured the beauty of the landscape. I was, frankly, afraid to go outside of Bloomington. I also came expecting the glorious blue quarries and the Cutters winning the bike race in *Breaking Away*. The quarries are now full of brackish water and toxic PCBs, and the police ticket anyone they catch swimming there. The original Little 500 Cutters are not the four townies portrayed in the movie *Breaking Away*, but a more upscale group of ex-frat boys who launched a tradition carried on by IU students.

Currently the Bloomington City Council is considering a proposal to ban smoking in public places. People have been writing letters to the editor, railing against the "do-gooder liberals" who want to control every facet of life. Pretty soon, one outraged letter writer wrote, these interfering do-gooders will see to it that you can't even eat unhealthy food if you want. Another letter writer pointed out that liberals are the reason we have those damned seatbelt laws. Another claimed he had a constitutional right to smoke; it was right there in the First Amendment. The letters go on and on, dripping with vitriol.

My native California friends ask me about Indiana. They want to know if it's beautiful or strange. I tell them it is both. For them, Indiana is "the East." Most of them have stopped asking me if I'm coming "home." After all, it has been seven years. I don't know if there are any statutes of limitations, but if there are, it is likely I am no longer a Californian, since my driver's license and my legal address now belong to Indiana. But then, neither am I a Hoosier.

The Redneck Gift

WHEN WE VISITED Connecticut for the holidays in 2000, my husband and I decided to move back to the United States. I say "back" because I was born in New York but left the country at the age of seven and never had the opportunity of visiting again. The move was going to be huge for us. We were going to face a different lifestyle and an unknown culture with a different language. I knew English well enough to manage, but my husband and oldest son knew only a little, and my youngest son, none at all. We believed we were making the right decision, that the United States would provide our children the possibility of having a better future. It didn't worry us at all that we would be starting all over in our forties, an age when almost everybody in the States is done starting over and is preparing to send their children to college.

The initial problems we needed to solve were where to live and how to support ourselves the first couple of months if we couldn't find jobs. My sister in Indiana and a friend in Connecticut offered us a place in their homes. So we had to make a big decision. Which place would be the best for our family to get adjusted to a very different way of life? After many family discussions, we finally decided that a small town would be the best thing for all of us. Why? Because we knew what life was like in a small city in Patagonia, and although we knew that Mount Vernon, Indiana, was ten times smaller than Puerto Madryn, we assumed its lifestyle would be pretty close to what we were accustomed to. Mount Vernon appeared to be a quiet and safe place where our children would be able to play outside alone without needing a fence to protect them, without us watching them all the time, and without being afraid of somebody stealing their bikes.

The decision was made, and we thought it would work out well, but at the precise moment we said that we had decided to try our new life in Indiana, warnings from everybody fell over us like heavy rain on a hot summer day in Buenos Aires.

"Indiana is a white state."

"Foreigners are not very well accepted, so be careful with your children at school."

"These people live in the middle of the land and think there's nothing beyond the cornfields."

"You must take care of your kids because people there have very little cultural background, and you don't want them to become 'rednecks.'"

The list of serious warnings was endless. Every single word mentioned to us would put down the "Hoosiers," a word I didn't know then, but which I now know is a term that identifies Indiana's inhabitants.

We heard not a single good thing about the people we were planning to have as our neighbors! My Lord, where are we going? Should we stay in Argentina and try to survive? And, by the way, what is a "redneck" after all? All these questions entered in our daily conversations. We also worried about our appearance because we come from European families; we have white skin and green-blue eyes. Do "rednecks" have red skin all year long or only in the summer because of the sun? Maybe if it was only a sun matter we were not going to look that different because we were arriving in winter. It wasn't going to be so bad; they wouldn't notice the difference if we didn't open our mouths.

Although we listened to what we were told, we didn't take these warnings as absolute truth because we both believed that everyone in this world can be his or her own person and that our behavior and our friendliness could make a difference. When we were young, nobody ever listened to classical music or went to ballet classes in our neighborhood, but our father and mother took my sister and me anyway telling us that "cultural knowledge" was the only real gift they could bequeath us, something nobody could take away from us. So we finally decided to make the move and started packing.

During the long process of packing the household, my father was the only person who encouraged us, who spoke positively about the people we were going to deal with. He had visited Indiana several times in the last nine years, staying for a couple of months each time. Before he retired, he had worked in a supermarket in Mount Vernon. His vision about people there was quite particular; he always found a positive thing to say about them: "They don't know how to socialize with people that are different from them but they really try when you take the first step. They're proud of their land and their history, and that is an outstanding quality that we don't have here in Argentina." He told us that people are the same everywhere and we would be fine if we faced things slowly, accepted new things, and had patience to be accepted ourselves. He added, "There are narrow-minded people everywhere, and you should try to avoid them no matter where you chose to live in. Just be yourselves and try to get along with them." His words were a relief that kept our hopes high.

We arrived in this little town in the middle of nowhere at the end of December in 2001. The weather was really cold for us, but not as bad as we thought it could be. Almost immediately we started on the paperwork we needed to start "being" in this country. The first thing we did was to apply for a social security number. It took three weeks to arrive. Without that number we could not take our driving tests because you're not allowed to apply for a driver's license if you don't have a social security number. We couldn't open a bank account because we didn't have a driver's license. We began to get gloomy, when suddenly the bank's vice president authorized me to open an account with my American passport until I got my number and driver's license. Huh! We passed the first obstacle because a "nice redneck" (that was what I was told about him) from the bank gave us a hand.

We also got help establishing credit. Americans are accustomed to establishing credit very early in their lives by asking for an extension of their families' credit card and that's it. But for someone who had never had credit in this country and is considered a "ghost," it's a long and hard road. You must have credit to get credit, and if you don't have it and you don't have a full-time job, nobody will "commit suicide" by giving you a loan. Although we had this against us, a car dealer (from whom we bought our first car in cash) heard our story and sent us to talk to somebody at the bank to ask for a loan. After a few interviews we got our first loan! It was on a CD we had to open in advance and deposit in it the same amount of money of the loan as collateral. A week later we found out that this car dealer was an important member on the board of the bank.

In the meantime, I was helping our children adjust in school, one in kindergarten and the other in fifth grade. We had chosen the small Catholic school in town, and we will never regret it because the whole staff worked to help our children learn the language and feel comfortable. The other students were great with them, too! The children's adjustment went well, and now, after a year here and actually going to public schools, I can say they're completely included in "Mount Vernon's school society."

My youngest son's teacher always says to me she admires how he is able to switch from one culture and language to the other one and respect both equally. If people around here were so narrow minded and closed as we were told, how can you explain all these demonstrations of interest and kindness toward us? It may be a gift from God, or maybe people from Indiana are trying to open up to the world after years of isolation and bad reputation among foreigners. And I include in the word "foreigners" other Americans also, because the bad reputation toward Indiana comes from them, too. You don't think people in Argentina know anything about Indiana, do you? The only image they could have of American farmers is if you tell them about the very popular television series in the sixties, *The Beverly Hillbillies*, an image that is pretty deplorable and, I believe, absolutely unfair.

In February 2002, I applied for a job as a ballet instructor, a job I had performed for many years in Argentina and I knew very well. The artistic director readily accepted me; however, I knew the problem was going to be in the class, with the students and their parents watching. Some fathers buy their outfits and their conversations showed they were shift-workers, or people without college degrees. The first day they saw me and heard me, I think they weren't very impressed with me as the new instructor. But after a year of teaching my classes and learning from each other how we approach life differently because of our cultures, I can tell you that some of them have become dear friends to me. I can feel their respect and their happiness with my progress in life. And you know what? I respect them very much, too, because they were able to pass the barrier of prejudgment and slowly accepted this new person with a strange accent and different behavior and manners. Wow! Is that too much for a "redneck"? Or is it that the names "rednecks" or "honkies," with which the "outsiders" tease them, are unfair?

My husband is an engineer. After six months of rejection, he finally found a job, thanks to one of my friends in the ballet studio. He got a labor job through a temporary agency very close to where we live. The manager of the agency went with him the first day to help with the paperwork and to introduce him. On the way to the factory he told my husband to be patient with his new boss because he was an authentic white, tattooed, bike-riding "redneck" who didn't like foreigners at all. Well, my poor husband arrived at the plant scared to death. But guess what? Every time my husband didn't understand something and asked the boss to repeat his instructions, this man did it. He spoke slowly so my husband could understand and didn't let him eat alone, always inviting him to sit among them for lunch. There were only two things wrong. Nobody could say my husband's name, "Guillermo," so they asked his permission to call him "G," to which he acquiesced, and when they all gathered for lunch, Guillermo never understood what they were talking about because they spoke too fast for him. However, even the "tough people" accepted his condition as a foreign Spanish-speaker and always showed him their respect.

One day, almost eleven months after we arrived, I was shopping for our first Thanksgiving in the States. I was staring at the boxes of pudding mix, not knowing which one to buy and if the dessert I was thinking about would taste the same as in Argentina. From the right side of the aisle came an old lady looking at the shelves like she was trying to find something. She stopped by my side.

"We never have enough for Thanksgiving, do we?"

"I don't know; this is my first one," I answered.

"Your first what, dear?"

"My first Thanksgiving."

She looked at me as if I was somebody from outer space.

"I mean," I explained, "I've only been in this country for eleven months, so this is our first celebration."

"Oh! So where are you from?"

"I was born in New York but raised in Argentina. I speak Spanish much better than English."

"Don't say that dear, you sound just like us, you look like one of us, so you are one of us now. I'm so glad to meet you." She introduced herself, Jean Newman, and told me about her husband, who was once the principal of Mount Vernon Junior High School. She said he was now very sick with an illness that kept him home for a long time. "Welcome to the States. If you need anything, just remember my name."

The conversation with this nice old lady made me really happy, and I went home and told everybody what had happened to me. When I mentioned that she said "you are just like us," one of my sister's relatives said, "Is it good to be 'just like us?'" I thought for a few seconds what she really meant with that question, and again all the awful things I'd been hearing about people around here came to my mind. I chose my thoughts to answer as carefully as I could, but I can't deny that her question made me mad. "Yes, I think it's good, and she made me feel home with her words. I liked what she said," I replied.

One day in a fellowship meeting in my church they were trying to figure out how to be better at welcoming people, and they asked me, while I was sitting quietly in my chair, how I felt about this matter. I spoke the truth, saying that it was so cold, that nobody talked to me for six months, that only the people from school said hello to me, and that I felt lonely but I accepted it because I didn't go to church to socialize but for something more important. The meeting froze while they stared at me speechless, and not a single whisper came out of their mouths. I understood they were not mad at me, but they were shocked because they had never realized how an outsider could feel among them. Slowly the oldest one spoke. I could feel her discomfort was huge. She had no idea someone could feel so lonely because of her ignorance. She was so sorry, she said, she couldn't even explain it. I stopped her and thanked her for being sincere and said we should all think together how to make the welcoming warmer for others.

These church ladies were acting like this because they didn't know how to behave better, and they thought their behavior was okay. They were absolutely stunned when they realized they were failing in their main purpose of fellowship and community spirit. After our conversation, they decided upon how to better welcome newcomers. We are still working on it.

After all these experiences I keep asking myself, why is this state so ridiculed by "outsiders"? Why is this but a flyover part of the country? Why are these people put down so harshly that they believe their accusers and even put themselves down? I guess in the history of the United States, these feelings were forged against the midwestern people, and they responded by closing the doors to outsiders and on and on. Both sides started a vicious cycle that continued for my family and me. We don't believe stories about "rednecks" anymore. We like it here, and we feel comfortable and accepted. We think our struggles to try to fit in are over. We are "inside" now.

My parents always taught me to be myself, to defend my ideals while respecting those of others, to be a good person, to find my gift, and to look for each person's gift because we all have one no matter how small it is. It's there inside us, and it only needs to be found. After a year living among them, we finally found out what the "redneck's" gift was. It was hospitality because they really made us feel at home.

Back Home in the City

"Tower'd cities please us then, And the busy hum of men."

JOHN MILTON

Harvesting the City

I LIVE IN Evansville, Indiana, the unofficial eastern frontier of the great bread-basket of the American Middle West. Formerly, boreal forests covered this land so thickly that, as the story goes, a squirrel could have hopped from Evansville to South Bend without ever touching the ground. Beneath the canopy suspended over tall walls of wood, the earth lay pretty much unbroken, except for the small patches of prairie in the midsection of what was to become a state. A cathedral of trees on the shore of an ocean of grass.

The forests have gone: that has been the price of our colonizing these river bends and fitting the forest to Hoosier farms. And, the crops—corn and soy—that are grown here more likely feed bovine than human populations. Our bread (typically white and flabby) is grown, kneaded, and packaged elsewhere; most of our vegetables come to us now from California or Mexico in semis that squeeze cars off the interstates. As we built our city we traded the trees for concrete and relinquished the satisfying of our most basic needs to others. It is no surprise, then, that cities are not healthful homes for us.

But I happen to live in this midwestern city. Outside of work and home, I spend many hours weekly as a volunteer at an inner-city social-service center, Patchwork Central. The center occupies the site of the original Jewish synagogue in town, now a corner in a crumbling part of Evansville. Friends and I work the land around Patchwork.

Across the street, a white house falls in on itself, windows boarded up and the front door barred. From the second story, a set of French doors opens onto

a drop of about fifteen feet to the row of hemlocks that we have planted as a
barrier. On what was the front porch of this century-old wood-frame building,
a charred mattress conceals cockroaches, while just outside the back door, a
discarded sofa makes a luxurious pallet for alley cats. The house has not been
vacant long; its last inhabitants were the hookers for whom the boarded-up
doors and windows made for maximum security. For them it didn't matter that
the balcony was missing from the second floor or that pigeons had moved into
the building through the holes in the soffit. But the prostitutes have gone, and
the house is crumbling in on its final tenants—pigeons, cockroaches, rats—the
ultimate inheritors of the city.

Next door, our garden occupies the space where a similar structure stood
until it was consumed by fire several years ago. (That is what happens to houses
in these Evansville neighborhoods. They lie vacant for a while, then go up in
smoke, usually in the middle of the most sweltering of summer nights, when
the air is so thick with wet that it takes palpable shape. Sirens blare, surprise you
from restless sleep, and you guess that another house has succumbed. This con-
summation by fire mocks the humid condition of summer weather here.) Then
the rubble sat for months until the city sent bulldozers in to raze the building,
scratching ancient alluvial soil over charred rafters and burnt bricks, which in
our garden today rise from their casual, unnatural graves between stalks of hol-
lyhocks or next to the red-flowering crape myrtles.

* * * *

The fate of this downtown lot will be different from that of the others.
Those lots sit idle but never vacant: discarded bags of chips cling, vengeful and
empty, to early weeds that crowd in the wake of a collapsed house or defunct
yard; hollow pop cans shine in the sun; bottles drained of their alcohol hide in
the slithering threes of poison ivy leaves; small plastic packages filled with catsup
or mustard spread out on the ground, not on a fast-food burger or fries. Layers
of paper wrap lie listlessly nearby, waiting for a wind to send them express to
another forgotten yard.

But this lot will not be idle; it has become the site of our garden. A friend
bought it for $450—which included $250 for the property and almost the same
amount for what are glibly called "lawyers' fees"—and gave it to us, members
of Patchwork Central, an intentional community. Part of our intention is to
work together—an exercise of moral responsibility and spiritual discipline—to

revitalize these decrepit neighborhoods; part of our understanding of community includes the notion that we live in close and complex connection with the land as we do with one another. And we have made this little land into an urban garden, a place where neighbors and we can stretch out or sit, a place where trees and birds are cared for, a place that blossoms and shelters in a city that does neither.

Creating the urban garden was not difficult. The main ingredients were money and lots of labor. Surprisingly, the money was not too hard to come by. I have worked to raise funds for some of the programs that our intentional community undertakes, I know how much we depend on what donors will give, and I have learned what language works in grants. What pleased me was the ease with which granting agencies were willing to support an urban garden program. With about $3,500 I was able to get six large trees—two sugar maples, two Norway spruces, and two white pines—along with a ring of dogwoods, white and pink. The row of hemlocks stands on a little berm (created with dirt excavated from what was to become the patio) separating our garden from the white house. Burning bushes follow the broken path of the sidewalk, protecting collections of crape myrtles, butterfly bushes, and nandina. In front of the patio are planted the most unusual specimens—a weeping cherry tree and a weeping mulberry, whose green coiffure swoops down to the ground. With the help of my friends, I put down two tons of flagstone in a path that connects Sixth Street and Blackford Avenue; we also yanked out railroad ties from along the alley and set them as a retaining wall for the hemlock hill. One leftover tie stands straight up, obelisk-like, an unusual position for one of these creosoted sleepers. It has become the towering support for our first birdhouse.

So we have meddled with the typical process of urban development and rendered this space unsuitable for human or business inhabitancy. Trees and stone pathways consume land that could support a house or business; we keep the created space free of trash, pull weeds, water when rains fail. No house will rise from the ashes of this fire.

Neither do we intend to return the lot to its recent prehuman past. Many years ago, before the original Americans settled in small agricultural communities alongside the river that was not yet called Ohio, huge oaks towered overhead, shading the forest floor so completely that few shrubs would grow, and the understory darkness was broken only where herds of woodland bison had trampled their way through in search of salt licks or the occasional outcrop of prairie grass to the north and west. (What I know of this history is not what I have learned from local old-timers or the lore of stories rooted in this place. A newcomer, I have had to turn to books and maps, the order of knowledge that comes *after* the intimate, tactile knowledge of soils and weather and the wide, subjective wisdom of the tellers of tales. To some degree, how we learn determines the sorts of things we know. I am learning now to touch and feel the knowledge that I gleaned from books.)

What we wanted to do was to create an attractive space where people and place could meet. Such a statement may seem absurd, yet it seems to me that— particularly in modern cities—Americans have little or no intentional connection with the land they inhabit or with the history of that land. This may appear ironic: surely Americans, of all peoples, recognize the natural legacy that this vast nation represents, surely Americans appreciate and make use of the country's natural abundance. But the story is different on a personal, daily level. (The truth is that we live in the archetypical breadbasket but do not make our own bread; we live in rich agricultural land but do not consume what we produce.)

We have learned to live apart from the rhythms and the rigors of the natural world: our homes are chilled (often unpleasantly frigid) in warm periods, we keep the thermostat high in winter, we are sheltered from winds and wet, we move from one artificial environment to the next as we live out our days. But shelter from the vagaries of the natural world should not necessarily mean *separation* from that world. While many people mow their lawns, few of us raise gardens—flowering beds, small crops of vegetables, planned plantings of trees and shrubs—and miss out on the physical, aesthetic, and spiritual benefits of such work. This work bears fruit, it involves us in intimate cycles of growth and dissolution, it ties us to the earth as we ingest leaves and fruits grown in the soil or as we sense beauty in what comes of the soil. Oddly enough, this work can serve as a lesson in humility too. Despite our best efforts, tomatoes sometimes wither and die; surprise late frosts lop off heads of beans or corn. Gardening offers an antidote to the popular notion that we can be self-sufficient individuals and that a measure of success in life depends on the degree to which we can control our environment. (Occasionally, the weather will still refuse to be controlled: the surprise March ice storm that downs power lines and keeps us trapped in our darkened homes, the June gale that blows hard on the heels of heavy rain and lifts trees from the ground as though they were twigs, or the 2003 winter that actually kept us seasonally and consistently cold and snowy.)

It is the culturally sanctified practice of land ownership that reifies the distance between human and natural worlds. As long as we think of land as something we can own, something that can be bought and sold, we will not be fully able to see and understand ourselves as part of the landscape, limited and mutable, ourselves without a price or a meaningful list of measurements (despite the résumés, CVs, test scores, and other "standardized" attempts to tag and label us), nor will we be able to see land as more than a "natural" resource—something that exists entirely for our use and for our benefit. (See how our language does dirty work for us, in this case attaching positive connotations of "natural" to what truly should read "self-serving.") Until we begin to see a relationship between ourselves and the land on which we live, we cannot see land as anything but exterior to us—and thus ownable. Our city neighborhoods comprise people and place; we need to recognize that we are all people of a *place.*

The distinction that our culture has drawn between ourselves and the land has bred, in many of us, contempt for the land. Because we have so little respect for the land, we don't complain when city crews come through and demolish healthy, aged trees (under the pretext that the trees may, at any time, fall on homes or vehicles in arboreal suicide). Because we take so little collective responsibility for how the land appears, we voice no concern when highways rip through city neighborhoods and in a stroke flatten homes and established yards or when living spaces are paved over with eyesore gas stations or strip malls. (How ugly are these tawdry, constructed oases of mercantilism, which proliferate and congregate along once-grand avenues, shouting out their names in penetrating lights throughout the night. Everywhere in the country, these citystretches are much the same: the brand names, the shape of the selling spaces, the look of the marquee define no place. With the exception of a token palm or two, these streets could be found in Tampa or Topeka.) This is the real landscape of our city spaces. It doesn't take a surrealist to see and lament, with Jean Baudrillard, "the desert of the real."

At the same time, we fail to acknowledge that land can have subtle, psychic dimensions in our lives. In an essay entitled "Place, Self, and Writing," Gerald Kennedy describes what he calls "interiorized terrains," the profound, affective attachments to the physical environment that humans make. Kennedy talks about the self-knowledge that comes about through our interaction with the houses we lived in; the neighborhoods we grew up in; the lawns, gardens, and trees of our daily and growing acquaintance. These are the landscapes of our most intimate experiences, and landscape continues to be linked—though suggestively or symbolically—to these experiences. (How does an urban field of empty chip bags and discarded bottles and cans translate into dreams? What symbolic construct comes of homes that immolate themselves or buildings that collapse from neglect?) The essay goes on to posit the "ontological status" of place—the recognition that, as people, we grow up in places that exist independent of—not as a function of—ourselves. These places inform—may even determine—our ideas of who we are; these places imprint onto the subconscious in the landscapes of dreams or the mystical fixtures of symbols. A rich and diverse landscape offers its human residents the natural stuff of dreams. In our garden in Evansville, we hoped that we could contribute something other than landscapes of cracked concrete or household ruin to the interior lives of neighborhood residents.

We also wanted to establish a natural landscape that might endure in a neighborhood that picks up and moves, the houses like revolving doors where people regularly come and go as relationships dissolve and household economies falter. (Many of the frame homes in inner-city Evansville were subdivided during the World War II years in order to accommodate a large influx of workers needed to build and operate the machinery of war. The upright, single-family homes built around the turn of the century by European immigrants became apartments, which now provide cheap housing for group homes, single-parent households, and other folks who cannot afford to get out.) This transience is not endemic to this neighborhood alone: Americans change homes and addresses frequently. Many people seem to think of the places that surround and house them as way stations on the acquisitive path to luxury or in the frenzied grab at the protean material advantages of modern life. (In their wisdom, traditional peoples assert that it takes a lifetime to know a place and to know yourself in context of that place. Theirs is the long view that comes from looking more closely, more intimately, and with more understanding at where they live. Theirs is the recognition that knowledge can be intensive—highly local, emotion based, and specific—as well as extensive.) Even when we are "settled" we are ever moving, shuttling from home to car to work to school and back, always sure that we need to be on the move, that our development as human beings parallels career or work-path change, that where we are can never say as much about ourselves as where we are going or where we would like to be.

* * * *

What is the landscape that we are envisioning—for Evansville and elsewhere? In his book *The Machine in the Garden*, Leo Marx expresses concern that

traditional American symbols of order and beauty have been divested of meaning, and I think that he is right. For Marx, there is no longer an ideal landscape
to which all Americans look or which they might collectively imagine: a shared
appreciation of bucolic landscapes and of the calm that such an environment
might betoken does not figure in the minds of people raised in a technological
age (or, for that matter, raised without cultivated connectedness to any place).
Marx would surely look aghast at the procrustean order of weedless green suburban lawns which, while apparently healthy and superficially appealing, bespeak
the bankruptcy of individual imagination (as they do the enriching of the chemical industry!). At the same time, we readily accept a city space filled with tawdry
shops, oceanic asphalt parking lots, and commercial glitz that scopes us out
as we drive. What frightens me most is that these cityscapes become the visual
standard on which we—and our children—are schooled. For the children in
the neighborhood of our garden, *clean* is a sidewalk free of debris and buckled
concrete; *fresh* is a sugared snack just unwrapped; *alive* is the noise of the traffic.
Their world provides little for a developing aesthetic sense. What that world *does*
provide is myriad references to things that can be bought, the constant and cor-
rupting advertising of goods most of us do not need or would not want were we
not programmed to desire them. For us, the "ideal" landscape is a living alternative to the waste of urban spaces, the anonymity of the suburban lawn, and the
earth-consuming onslaught of commercial development.

So we recognize the need to create beautiful spaces in the city—and to care
for those spaces. In an essay entitled "Building Dwelling Thinking," Martin Heidegger states that caring for the places we inhabit becomes an important part
of our maturation as humans. As we grow to care more deeply and more finely
for each other, so too do we grow in our ability to cherish and care for the land
that succors us and the houses that shelter us. His observation is borne out by
the words and practices of traditional peoples throughout the world. Traveling in Zimbabwe, I visited Victoria Falls, named (for Western posterity) by the
nineteenth-century missionary-explorer David Livingstone for the queen under
whose auspices he was traveling. I learned, however, that Shona-speaking local
people—who had long preceded Livingstone in his "discovery"—called the cata-
ract "the cloud that thunders" in their language, an appellation alive with wonder
and metaphor in a language that regularly links human and natural worlds. Their
naming of the place proceeds from—and reflects—reverence for their environment, while the European label for these falls is full of political and imperial
implications. It is a telling difference. "Building Dwelling Thinking" goes on to

show that only by living in close and caring relationship with a particular place can humans learn, ironically, to be most sentiently human. An existentialist, Heidegger would say that observation of the impermanent and changing natural world teaches humans little about selfhood but much about modesty, and it is modesty that characterizes the people attuned to their place in the world.

* * * *

Ironically, I must admit that I feel a foreigner to this medium-sized city in the inconvenient boot of Indiana. My affinity lies with knobby hills clothed in second-growth oak and hickory trees of Appalachian hollows where the clayey soil is rocky, the undergrowth scrubby. The flat floodplains in this town may be nutrient rich but lack the surprise natural variety of the Ohio hills I grew up in. Despite its reputation as an agricultural state, Indiana is densely populated, and the early waves of European settlers to this region blotted out forests and continue to keep hedgerows (where striking daylilies, gnarled hazelnut trees, and the magical bittersweet vine can thrive) unnaturally clean and cropped; little forest remains; the landscape is everywhere domesticated. Mostly, though, the difficulty has been an acceptance of city environments, where the sagging roofline of my neighbor's house marks the western horizon, and it is the sound of police sirens that rouses us in the mornings. I am not by choice a city dweller.

But I have adopted this place and I call it my home, though it has been a slow process of finding a place for myself in Evansville. I have embarked on a process of what Wes Jackson calls "becoming native to a place," which, for him, implies becoming part of a community that is responsible to the ecological implications of the surrounding world. It is a deliberate and at times difficult move. My first years here I felt alien to the land and what it produced. The city grid affronted my sense of aesthetic variety; strip malls crowd in where houses and neighborhoods fall; the fickle weather can vary from tropical to polar in a matter of weeks. At one point, my wife and I vowed that we would leave our pleasant home if another tree were removed from our block. Despite the indignation that accompanied the extirpation of the black oak across the street, we stayed. Other trees have fallen since then.

But we stay. We have become part of a community, and as a group of people we have adopted Evansville as our yard, our collective homestead, and we have taken some responsibility for redressing social and ecological injustice. We do not hold to the values of Thomas Jefferson, who believed that, in America, the ideal civilized life would take place on well-run garden farms, the "gentleman farmer" a kind of enlightened, benevolent despot. We recognize that much of the world lives in cities, and much of the rest is busy moving toward urban centers. We recognize too that Jefferson's dream had its origin in a classist society where there would be a large corps of laborers willing to work for little in keeping places attractive for the use of others. For all its obvious limitations, our landscape is more democratic.

* * * *

Part of our motivation is to improve—if only in the smallest of ways—the aesthetic scape of the neighborhood in which we work, one characterized by high unemployment, generalized poverty, and transiency. Ours is not a romantic view of a beneficent natural environment that, if left to its own devices, encourages healthy human growth. The history of agriculture is a story of the interaction of human need and the occasional compliance of the natural world; our garden sits on this frontier, which represents the site of important learning for all of us. Few children in these dirty city blocks know that the french fries they eat each day come from anywhere other than freezer-proof plastic bags. The kids that participate in our garden programs, however, have sliced and planted fleshy potato eyes in March; pushed soil over the furrows; watched plants emerge, flower, and die back; returned in June to dig the fat fleshy tubers; and pared and cooked and consumed the fruit of the soil and of their labor. It is easy to underestimate the importance of this lesson—in the interconnectedness of food and human, in the mystery of growth and subterranean development, in the picking and preparation of what nourishes our bodies, in the relation between caring and need, in the appreciation of the growing beauty of the plants and of the smell and taste of the fruit. These activities and this learning have taken place here, in this small garden on a revitalized city lot.

Work in our garden complements other work for which members of our community take responsibility: we run after-school tutoring and art programs for kids, sponsor the Neighborhood Economic Development Center, staff and manage the Emergency Food Pantry, organize reading programs and bike-riding sessions and so on. We care for the neighborhood as we care for its residents and for ourselves. That care is work, and we consider this work a sort of spiritual exercise, one that binds humans to one another, to the places where they are together, and to forces that precede and follow after us in life. It is not an easy exercise: favorite neighbors suddenly move away, vandals smash plants or outdoor artwork, we have to fight to keep the vision of a potential garden in this American city alive and growing in our minds, we cannot be deterred by continued collapse of homes and lives around us or by the apparent success of the prevailing American dream—where everything (so the thinking goes) can be bought, briefly enjoyed, and discarded.

In Evansville, the pigeons hover, ready to roost in the homes people have vacated; rats wait for the trash to accumulate behind neglected buildings. What we have discovered, however, in the harvest of our labor, is how richly productive the city soil—once uncovered and cared for—can be.

Taking Up Residence

RECENTLY, ONE OF MY sisters overheard our children sparring about the tenets of their individual identities. They were talking about where they had been born, what school received their allegiances, which one had the coolest toys and best friends. At one point they debated whether being born in Virginia, as they had recently discovered about their grandmother, meant you weren't an American, but instead a child of some other country. My sister's son, the eldest in that generational tribe, boasted that regardless of his grandmother's nationality, at least she was a Buckeye. My daughter answered defensively, "Well, we're Buckeyes too!"

Looking at my daughter, but speaking to me, my sister settled the debate. "No, honey, you are a Hoosier. Even your mom's a Hoosier now."

The conversation struck me as funny at the time, insightful a few days later when I thought again about the motive for my sister's clarification. Of the three girls in my family, I'm the one who moved away. I'm the one who took off after high school and then struck out for the foreign territories of Kansas and Mexico and eventually the permanently foreign world of academia. I'm the one with the thinnest vein of courage, but the only one with a passport. And I'm the one who has to travel back frequently to maintain my identity as a native rather than a visitor among my family of origin. My sister is right—I am a Hoosier, not a native but an immigrant.

My house in Anderson is nearly one hundred years old, but I've lived in it only eight years. In that span of time, though, my family has made its mark on the property. We've transformed the backyard, reduced the flower beds to more manageable gardens, added a large swing set for the kids, and replaced the awful evergreen bushes in front with a rose of Sharon on one side and a purple Chinese plum on the other. We've altered the interior, too. Starting with the top floor and working our way down, we've repainted every wall and ceiling, stripped and refinished the wood floors, remodeled the basement, and replaced the carpet everywhere but in our children's bedrooms. Last winter, we even added an oak firebox and gas logs.

I don't know whether the family that lived here before us would be impressed or grieved by the changes we've made. They lived in this house at the corner of High Street and Cottage Avenue for twenty-three years, retiring to Savannah, Georgia, when their health simply couldn't endure another Indiana winter. I don't know whether they would view our renovations as improvements, but I'm certain they would acknowledge our ownership. They would say with certainty, "That's not our house anymore." I like to think my family's presence is overt and audible, that friends recognize our house because they recognize our hand-prints pressed all over it.

The house across Cottage Avenue, however, is a kind of turnstile, a station through which new residents flow every spring. The house contains three apart-ments, a three-room space on the first floor, a narrow one-bedroom upstairs, and an invisible apartment somewhere in the rear of the building. I've been inside the front apartment, and my son plays almost daily with a little boy who lives in the upstairs unit. But my only knowledge of the couple that currently occupies the rear is the occasional glimpse I have of them getting into or out of a large blue van. The young woman hauls a baby carrier over one elbow, a gigan-tic diaper bag creating balance on the opposite shoulder. So I wonder, situated across the street from a house whose residents seem to have no true territory, what is it that makes my claim of this corner any less tentative than the families that pass through the rooms next door? What makes me think my identity as an emigrated Hoosier or my twenty-year residence in Anderson is any more perma-nent than the pauses my neighbors make here?

High Street and all its short tributaries are dotted with rental properties. Most of the houses on the south side of the street are beat-up, squarish houses inhabited by college students. The homes on all of the cross streets are similarly worn: shaggy grass, peeling yellow paint, and cluttered front porches. A few of the properties along this three-block, downhill stretch are family residences, but most of the houses in my neighborhood are owned by people who don't live in them. And the people who do live there don't spend much time mowing the grass or repairing broken shutters. Like water in a shallow stream, my neighbors trickle by on a steady, predictable current.

Perhaps my preoccupation with the house across Cottage Avenue is the static quality of its face. Other than the annual residue of someone's departure—a broken toy left in the yard or a pile of trash heaped on the curb by the landlord—the house never changes. It bears only the wear of traffic, not the maintenance of habitation. The truest reason for my preoccupation with the house across the street, however, is the consistency with which its occupants become a part of my life. Every summer since we moved to High Street, at least one of the units in that house has held a child close in age to one of my children. Typically, my son or daughter recognizes the new neighbor from school. Or the children eye one another from opposing curbs until one or the other thinks of something particular to say, a rope to toss across the unfamiliarity that separates them. As soon as one of them makes the crossing, they are friends, and I gain another set of hands reaching for Popsicles or bologna sandwiches.

"Let them come here," my husband says, "so you can keep your eye on them." He's right, of course. I can't trust the adults in the house across the street because I don't know them. I'll never know them well enough to let my children walk unselfconsciously through their doors because the families will move before summer rolls around again. I can't even trust the children to play safely or observe basic rules of courtesy. They ask for food, cry when it's time to go home, and sometimes steal money from my children's bedrooms. When the neighborhood children are visiting, anything can happen. My only guarantee is that in April, a new family and another smiling, needy child will want to play in my backyard.

And yet, the families that live in the house across the street mark my memory with dark, inky strokes. One of my daughter's friends lived in the front apartment with her mother and sister. Every time she stepped onto my front porch, I felt a piercing impulse to shelter her. I wanted to wash away the make-up and hair spray and get to the little girl cocooned in there—pierce the armor and then protect the tender skin inside it. A few months ago, the twelve-year-old boy in the upstairs apartment rang our doorbell with a request to use the phone. An hour and half later, I realized he was huddled outside his house, trying to stay warm and fill his boredom with any distraction. He spent that Sunday afternoon and evening with us, waiting eight hours for his mother to come home.

Of all the tenants who have occupied the house across the street, none have marked my life as distinctly as one family that lived in the front apartment for about six months. During one of our spring garage sales, this new set of neighbors came over to sift through boxes of baby clothes and toys in our driveway. The woman held a baby against her hip, and her son burrowed through the boxes marked *25 cents*. Eventually they approached me to pay for their selections. I added a quick total in my head and asked the woman when her family had moved into the house across the street.

"No hablo inglés. ¿Cuánto dinero para este?"

I wonder what my face said to her. *She speaks no English,* I thought. *My new neighbor speaks absolutely no English.*

"¿Cuánto?" she asked again.

Uno, dos, tres, cuatro. . . . The *Sesame Street* song jingled in my head. "Cuatro dólares," I answered.

She handed me her money, gathered her children, and turned away.

"Gracias, Señora. Buenos días," I called, exhausting my Spanish vocabulary.

By noon, my neighbor and her two boys were in my backyard, eating hot dogs and smoked sausages I had grilled for my family and the others who had pitched in for the garage sale. I can't imagine why she accepted my awkward invitation to eat with us, except that she was starving. Not for the sandwiches or cold sodas, and certainly not for an opportunity to teach her unilingual neighbors a few Spanish phrases. She was starving for company. Daily she swept the narrow concrete porch or sat at the step watching her son toss a ball around the yard. And I'd seen them rounding the corner on their way to or from a walk around the block. But in the weeks that they had occupied the house across the street, not a single friend had come to visit or play.

She stayed for an hour or so. We worked at conversation the way toddlers work at play, neither one knowing exactly how to communicate with the other person. Somehow I managed to learn the names of everyone in her family, the age of her baby, their location before moving to Anderson, and the length of time they had been in the United States. I think she asked me if there were any Spanish congregations in town, and I think I told her about St. Mary's, a Catholic church on 11th Street with a high population of recent Mexican immigrants.

In the weeks that followed, Berta and her two boys took up residence in my life. She and I kept working at conversation. The effort to communicate with her resurrected my college Spanish lessons. As my youngest son grew out of his pajamas and baby clothes, I took them across the street in grocery sacks.

And every day that it wasn't raining, her son banged through my back door yelling the name of my son or some other phrase that he used to identify me. Months later, after the family had moved to another run-down apartment on a more dilapidated street, I discovered that he was calling me Sabrina. In fact, the whole family identified me as Sabrina because Berta had mistaken (or misremembered) that as my name after our first meeting.

My name was only one of many things we misunderstood. One morning in June, Berta asked me to take her to the welfare office so she could register for food stamps. Her husband used their car to travel to jobs all over central Indiana, so during the day she had no means of transportation. We ran that errand first, piling our five children into my Durango. Then I asked if she needed to go anywhere else. She needed a few groceries, she told me, and a pair of tongs for cooking the tamales she sold at St. Mary's every week. We found a large pair of tongs at a housewares shop near the welfare office. By then the kids were getting hungry and bored, so I drove to Gene's Rootbeer Stand for ice cream cones. While we waited for the cones, Berta tried to tell me that she wanted something, wanted to go somewhere with me. Something about swimming, or maybe taking a shower. And then she asked me where she could get a big can of beans. We bantered for a few minutes, and finally I decided she needed commercial sized cans of refried beans for her tamales.

So we ran all over town looking for the beans. But every time we got into the aisles that had the jumbo-sized pickle jars and twenty-four count toilet paper packs, she shook her head and walked the other direction. Finally, in Gordon's Food Service, we turned a corner into an aisle of professional cookware. Her face lit up and she reached for a gleaming stockpot on the top shelf. A $65.00 gleaming silver stockpot. She yelped, "Aye!" and recoiled as if she might be charged just for touching it. A big pot. All afternoon she had been looking for a big pot, and all afternoon I had been trying to get her to buy beans. I could have taken her back to Meijer for a twelve-dollar stockpot, but I was too tired. Our children were sweaty in the rear seats, and my head throbbed from the process of constant, obviously incompetent, translation. When we got home, I gave Berta the stockpot from my own cupboard and called it a day.

This woman may spend the rest of her life in the United States, but chances are she will never spend more than a few months in one place. The frequency of her movement, though, is the one thing that keeps her from being entirely alien in this city. In the 1950s General Motors held an invincible, imposing presence in Anderson culture. A typical dinner-table question for a high school senior was, "So, are you going to college or going to work for GM?" By the 1980s, the company's stronghold began to deteriorate. Today people live in Anderson, but they work someplace else. Residents still work for GM, but when jobs go, they have to follow. They may leave Anderson reluctantly, but they still leave. The city is also populated by people who were not raised here. Yes, some residents built their lives around the security and eventual retirement from one of the two GM plants. However, many of the working adults who shape the economy of this area moved into the community after establishing themselves professionally and financially in some other city.

Madison County's rural landscape is transforming, too. Duane Rhule, a retired GM manager and longtime Indiana resident, lives on the farm where he was born. However, he has not spent his entire life there. Like most Americans, he moved several times within the United States and then spent four years in Australia. He rooted himself in his childhood soil only after leaving it for a while. But farmland no longer has the same depth or span it has in his memory. "People are bringing suburban ideas out of the city and imposing them on farm country," he says. "I see a loss of courtesy and respect for space, a loss of knowledge of neighbors. The houses are closer together, but we're all strangers." Urbanization may be to blame for the diminished size and shape of individual farms, but a lifestyle of restlessness keeps us moving. In this time and in this place, we grow more like ground cover than trees: shallow roots moving across our geography rather than down into the places we inhabit.

For about a year, I maintained a persistent friendship with Berta. She told me things that broke my heart, and she made me laugh with pantomimic descriptions of her fifteenth birthday party in Mexico or her days alone with the two boys. She wept on my couch one afternoon, trying desperately to reach her family in Mexico with a prepaid $10.00 phone card. Her mother was very ill. Her brother—or maybe an older son, one who didn't accompany her to the United States—was missing. She asked me to take her to a free health clinic so she could get birth control pills. In the lobby, we struggled with the personal information sheet. Entertaining our babies on the dirty floor, I winced at the first few questions, then braved up and just ignored the embarrassingly intimate nature of the details. Are you using contraceptives now? What kind? Have you ever had an abortion? Do you have any sexually transmitted diseases?

I'm still astonished that she hung with me all that time. And I wonder if my awkward gifts to her—the bags of clothes, the pile of wrapped presents on her front stoop in December, the roses I cut from my ragged flower garden—were gestures that she accepted as sincere friendship. I hope there was no pity in my giving. And I hope there was no shame in her acceptance.

Her family has moved again. A couple months ago, I found an invitation wedged in the screen on the back door. *Sabrina y niños* was written on the envelope. The card invited us to a birthday party for her son and included a phone number and an address. Unfortunately, I lost the card just a few weeks after the party, which we were not able to attend. And her son, a second grader now, left a phone message for us recently, but I haven't returned the call yet. Every time I catch the name and number in my peripheral vision, I tell myself that I need to call. I need to find out where they live now, arrange to visit them. And every time, I'm fatigued by that impulse. Maybe tomorrow, I think, when I have more time.

The truth is that my friendship with Berta requires something from me that no one else has ever demanded: intense attention and patience. I have to work hard at every conversation and forgive daily the minor inconveniences she and her children create in my life. And I have to fight my own arrogant desire to save them. The truth is that I dread resuming that connection. My language skills are rusty again, and my daily schedule is naturally full without them. Still, the distance I've placed between us is my loss more than it is hers. Other people have taken up residence in her life and daily enrich her vocabulary, her perceptions, her religious faith, and her knowledge of Indiana and its residents. For a while we were neighbors; that proximity expanded my view of the neighborhood.

Every day, my children ask me difficult questions: questions about God and war, questions about insects and storms, questions about sin and grace. Yet, if one of them asked, "Mommy, why don't we have any other friends like Berta and José?" I might not be brave enough to tell them the truth: because crossing cultures is more difficult than crossing the street, because paying attention takes so much time, because these new friends might move away when we aren't looking.

The man who currently lives in the house across the street is lonely and mentally ill, with a speech impediment so severe his sentences are nearly indiscernible. And the little boy in the upstairs apartment wears the same clothes three days in a row. His feet are always dirty, and his left eye crosses slightly when he looks down. Yesterday, he came around the corner wearing a heart-breaking grin, his bicycle helmet sitting crooked on his blonde head, the right bicycle pedal wiggling loose again. And I know it will be work to have him in my life. I'll have to insist that my son not close his bedroom door when they are playing in there. And I'll fix a lot of extra sandwiches and cups of Hawaiian Punch this summer. But if I shut him out, insisting on an ambivalent distance from the temporary residents in the house across the street, that house might never be a home. And the privacy fence around my yard will be just one more wall keeping strangers in and strangers out.

Perhaps transience is exactly what we have in common. Perhaps that is the white line that leads us continually across the street in search of one another. I moved to Anderson almost twenty years ago, expecting to stay long enough to gain an education and make a few new friends. But this city and the university where I live and teach has become magnetized, the gravitational center of my life's orbit. When I travel to Ohio for a visit with my parents, my children know we're almost there when they see a set of long, green-roofed barns just a few miles from Grandma's house. I know I'm almost home when I ease into the glare of Scatterfield Road, and then, thirteen stoplights later, cross the rumble strips on University Boulevard. Though I cannot imagine leaving this new homeland, the next twenty years of my life could take me somewhere else. From the perspective of the earth, my neighbors and I have the lifespan of a leaf, not a tree. Isolated, ignorant of one another's names and daily habits, we make no noise, mark the wind with only the slightest color. In community, we break the endless sky and sing an ocean in the trees. When the house across the street fills with new residents, I have two choices: remain invisible or be known. When new students surge through the campus valley like a young river, I can avoid the swell or get wet. The transient quality of this culture inspires me to find a stable bottom. What keeps me rooted in this place—Anderson, Madison County, central Indiana—is knowledge of the other people who are only passing through. Our only defense against the impermanence of our place in this landscape is to spend our season in the company of other leaves.

The Saintly and the Sinful:
Visions of Indiana Cities

BY BIRTH, I'M not a Hoosier. When August Alblinger, the pneumatic ex-seminarian from Schuttern, Germany, left his Bavarian hometown for a fresh start in the New World, it was on a forested bend of the Embarras River in eastern Illinois that he established his dynasty of seven children, not the Wabash, the White, or the Tippecanoe. I grew up in my great-grandfather's state with the certainty that Illinois had the greater claim to Lincoln, that we could boast what was then the second largest city in the country, and that hailing from "The Inland Empire" placed me a notch higher on some international scale of geographic status. A few opinions rang true as faith. Hoosiers were hicks; Illini were refined.

But living in the relative obscurity of southern Illinois, as remote from the kingdom of Chicago as from New York or Paris, our next-door neighbor Indiana always occupied our imaginations with its college towns and covered bridges, its limestone quarries and national forests. All of our news came to us from Terre Haute, the capital of the Wabash Valley, and I grew up knowing more about the Italian festivals in Clinton, the ups and downs of the basketball team at ISU, and the hoodlums "terrorizing" the streets of Linton, than I did about the goings-on of my native state. I loved the way the exotic names of Indiana towns slid off my tongue: Loogootee, Dugger, Switz City. The dry towns nearby were not nearly as chic or poetic: Oblong, Robinson, Willow Hill. Even our own town, Sainte Marie, seemed especially chaste and ecclesiastical, despite its French provenance and our Catholic penchant for beer. I longed to sail off

for Indiana's Scotland and Lebanon, to catch the sights in Orleans or Milan, to
tour its Brazil and Peru.

All that we didn't have, Indiana seemed to have. Even a piece of our heritage had been ceded to Indiana. When the Sisters of Providence from Ruille-
sur-Loir, France, headed off to establish their community in Sainte Marie, they
met a petulant Wabash River that had flooded its banks and, with a little coaxing
from the Bishop of Vincennes, they set up their order on the Indiana side of the
river, where they eventually built their pristine little college of gables and spires
today known as St. Mary-of-the-Woods. But they had sent ahead of them a set
of exquisite stained-glass windows that the town founders, once spurned, were
reluctant to return. In an act of hubris, these aristocratic Alsatian immigrants
built a pillared estate, their own miniature Versailles, in which they displayed
those stained-glass windows like spoils of war. Yet despite the town's defiance, its
eastern rival had won. All hopes of utopia went the way of the stagecoach, and
they settled down to life in a provincial village that would never come close to
being a city.

What's in a state? Can the same land, gouged and flattened by the same
glaciers, bear forth harvests in separate measures? Can the same soil seed different accents, the same wind bleach a cheek here and burn it there? To us,
the differences were clear. Downstate from Chicago, the humble farmsteads of
southern Illinois simmered in anonymity. But Indiana had succeeded in weaving a mythology around itself that drew a larger imagination to its tidy towns
and homespun version of Americana. How many movies had captured Indiana
vistas? We'd seen them all, from *My Gal Sal* and *Raintree County* to *Breaking Away*
and *Close Encounters of the Third Kind*. Indiana brought to the screen the kind
of Midwest the world wanted. It was the America that immigrants had longed
for, the land where they could transplant their folktales, the high ground where
they could worship freely, and the river-fed valley where they could raise a family and corral them close. Illinois got on with its business; Indiana lollygagged
in its rich past. No wonder Indiana birthed not such utterly knowable figures as
William Jennings Bryan and Ronald Reagan, but evasive luminaries like James
Dean and John Dillinger. Not commie rat Burl Ives or iconoclast Betty Friedan,
but prophetic Kurt Vonnegut and dapper Bill Blass.

Everything, it seemed, happened in Indiana. Weary of town square hab-
erdasheries and outdated five and dimes, we piled into the station wagon and
headed to Honey Creek Square Mall in Terre Haute, where Meis and Roots supplied our woeful wardrobes, and the Goodie Shop and Laughner's Cafeteria fed

us delicious treats. We got our pimples examined and our wisdom teeth extracted in Indiana. We took field trips to memorials of George Rogers Clark and Tony Hulman. Peaches waited for us each August in Vincennes; muskmelons rose in massive heaps at roadside stands all up and down Route 41. And when our larders lacked, we ate our most elegant meals at Evansville's Executive Inn or Win Schuler's in Fort Wayne. This was a state whose local charms hadn't been hogged by its largest city, and we gazed into the road atlas at a map of Indiana glittering with cultural gems.

Even our passions took a day trip to Indiana to get satisfied. When rumors chuffed around church circles about a certain confirmed bachelor, the ambiguity was always easily resolved with a curious euphemism: "Terre Haute on the weekends." Like our own little Las Vegas or Tijuana, this border town was purportedly the place to get a quick fix or trim a wild hair, and as a boy I envisioned alleys strung with clotheslines, prostitutes out on back stoops for a smoke, and lithe young men buttoning up as they slinked back to moral Illinois. I thought of slot machines and blackjack tables, drunken brawls, and gunshots fired into the night. To me, even San Francisco's streets weren't half as tough. Whether what I'd heard was true—whether Terre Haute came even close to Gomorrah—didn't matter. Lying awake to the static of cricket chirps rising from our dim backyard, I lived the hopeful fiction of what I was sure lay in store for me just across the Wabash.

Terre Haute. My first city. My first taste of the world. Terre Haute was a town where you weren't limited to the single pair of Toughskins on the rack at Gene's Menswear, where you could drive up and down wide, welcoming streets and never run out of restaurants or watering holes. A city with stoplights, parking meters, and pollution. In Vincente Minnelli's 1958 postnoir classic *Some Came Running*, Terre Haute plays off like a gritty industrial town with endless allure and more than a little danger. The kind of city you entered through strands of chintz beads, where the locals put their hands over their pockets just to be safe. Smothering in fabled Parkman, Indiana, a whitewashed, Bible Belt burg only Hollywood could dream up, Shirley MacLaine hangs on Frank Sinatra's arm, a tenacious floozy in a ratty boa, begging him for just one weekend in Terre Haute. When they finally do escape, Terre Haute provides a nervous, Cinemascopic backdrop to the drama, where she can slouch into her cocktail, croon a silky chorus of "After You've Gone" with some natty local boys, and, at least for awhile, derail Sinatra's plans of restoring his good name.

In all my trips there, I never found that Terre Haute. No starlets stepping off at bus stops, no avenues milling with GIs on leave, not even a single speakeasy with its flickering neon sign and aging patrons who remembered "the days." I never once glanced a jaw square enough to seduce Shirley MacLaine or knuckles white enough to do her in. By the time I made it there, strip malls and smorgasbords had supplanted lawless postwar debauchery. You could stuff your gut on the endless buffets at Duff's, but you couldn't find a brothel or a craps table to save your life. Still, I longed for what had once been, scrutinized the faces of its citizenry with almost scientific attention, determined to see in an eye or the crease of a smile the streetwise self-satisfaction of the city dweller. Unsure of my own sex, I wanted to know what Terre Haute could do for bachelors, what sins I could leave in its gutters, and I imagined my own weekend visits, a well-heeled single gentleman in a tailored suit and down-turned porkpie hat sailing into town to reap the treasures of this great city in the east. For all our merits, we had no such city in Illinois. We were an oversized province the world could ignore. Indiana, at least, was a state that made you look.

Still, I never figured I would find a life in Indiana, that the rustic fairy tales I'd eaten up as a boy would draw me there as an adult. When I went looking for a city, the only place I figured I could really be myself, I looked farther afield, past the flatlands to the more storied, forward-thinking states of the East Coast. If going east to Indiana could save me from a childhood all too chaste and quaint, why stop there? I studied maps of Boston, Washington, and Baltimore. I pondered Providence, Atlanta, and Miami. Scheming my certain exodus, I sent applications to graduate schools in Massachusetts, New York, Virginia, and just a few out west for good measure. But fate will take its course, old stories will take hold, and it makes strange and perfect sense that my next real city, perhaps my last city, would also be in Indiana.

I had been to Indianapolis before, and I knew from my high school geography book that it was the largest city in the country not founded on a navigable body of water. A planned city, the Midwest's Washington, D.C., Indianapolis hadn't just happened. It wasn't the promised land of pilgrims or the last resort of rogue settlers evading debtors. As such, it lacked the kind of cheeky charisma of Terre Haute or the typical cities I'd seen on television in shows like *CHIPS* or *Barney Miller*. Nary an overpass or bridge was marred with graffiti; no broken glass adorned its curbs. Indianapolis was a civic gem, a scrubbed-clean sentinel set in the center of a proud state that wanted to show only its best features to the world.

My first real trip to the city came in the eighth grade, when a few select students earned a weekend in Indianapolis with their good grades. Ms. Ward, a well-read teacher's aide hired to keep the restless "gifted" students busy, would be our guide. The one true sophisticate I knew in an institute of dunces, she spoke of art museums, English gardens, cute cafés, and, of course, fast, expensive cars. Blue eyes sparkling through blue-tinted reading glasses, this woman who had traveled to Europe and Asia made Indianapolis seem the center of the world, though we inquired why we had to leave the state. "Chicago?" she dismissed us. "Indianapolis will do much better." And it was closer, and it was safe enough for a band of eighth graders who knew little beyond their parents' farms.

Her tour-book version of Indianapolis proved largely true. We caravanned across the sleepy plains of Illinois, past Terre Haute (I gave a glance), over Hoosier cornfields and desolate acreage, through the gentle hubbub of interstate towns, and the city's skyscrapers rose a sudden wonder in otherwise unspectacular terrain. I had seen this same skyline in every Sunday night episode of *One Day at a Time*, seen the streams of traffic cruising through the city on a knot of highways, but the impact of its size and grace went well beyond the high-rise where unmarried Bonnie Franklin tamed her teenage girls. This Emerald City touched the sky! In Indianapolis, I learned a city was not just its sins but its virtues, too, and I put aside my taste for grit and fell in love instead with urbane artifice, with gilt and glint. In its own way, Indianapolis could connect me to the beauty I had read about in poetry and novels. We met van Gogh and Gauguin at the Indianapolis Museum of Art, we strolled through well-trimmed plots in Holcomb Gardens, we watched real jets take off and disappear into the ether, and we sang along to songs from the Wurlitzer organ at the Paramount Music Palace, no small-town pizza joint, to be sure. We even sinned a bit, staying up well past our bedtimes back home playing raucous poker games with Ms. Ward and telling off-color jokes or listening to her stories of Roman baths and Paris discos. All of this was allowed in the city, under Ms. Ward's permissive charge, and I felt a quiet sympathy for this woman who had sacrificed the world for the kids of Jasper County, Illinois.

As I grow older, I take comfort that I ended up in a city I have known for so long. My passage here brought with it little struggle, and my life in Indianapolis has been one of relative ease. In this confederacy of small towns, where nothing seems too large or convoluted, life is not far removed from the farms where so many people here were raised, the immigrant homesteads where they dreamed of something more. I am one of them; we share the privilege of this overgrown village. But I've not lacked for little of a typical metropolitan experience in the capital of Indiana. In this city, I've been robbed, I've wrecked a car at a gridlocked intersection, I've been threatened by beggars. I've seen men lingering in alleys and no trace of women, I've slinked home late a little drunk from clubs, I've learned of love in all-night diners and lost it just as quick in the light of day. Here, too, I've heard a hundred accents both frantic and charmingly placid. I've dined on spring rolls and pollo con mole, corn dogs and local lamb chops. And I've lived a few good stories of the city's past: its streetcars and canals, its ethnic neighborhoods, its jazz clubs overfilling Indiana Avenue.

But living well in Indianapolis comes not from its colorful treasures or even a composite of all its charms. It is not its race cars. It is not its major league teams. It is not its breaded pork tenderloins served in makeshift jail cells at the Tin Star or from a stand at the state fair. Not its symphonies or galleries. Not even its shy, polite people evading my stares. It is the access to all of these things without the rigor of larger cities and the quiet recognition that this could actually happen so far away from sanctioned civilization. And despite the ribbing I might receive from friends in larger places, I know that I do as much or more of city living in Indiana than I might anywhere else. No taking for granted what we have a fragile toehold on here in the Midwest, no neglecting our regional gifts.

I have learned one thing from all of my years as an urbanite: a city is nothing if not myth. New York sleeps; Chicago settles down. No matter the city one lives in, it's the way the city lives inside or issues forth, infecting the voice, inoculating one's tone. As such, Indianapolis is my story and poem, my sermon, my psalm. My anecdotes of late night crowds at the Chatterbox, of celebrity sightings, of parties filled to burst with friends. To my more worldly detractors, I can, like Ms. Ward, make Indianapolis seem the focus of the known universe.

The poet C. P. Cavafy, whose adopted Alexandria would forever satisfy his metropolitan lusts, once wrote, in response to a young friend filled with wanderlust: "You will age in the same neighborhoods; and you will grow gray in these same houses. Always you will arrive in this city. Do not hope for any other." Living in Indianapolis doesn't mean not hoping for any other. I still dream of eastern cities and their celebrated monuments, of the Venice I have visited once, the London I have not. I want for subways, channel boats, trolley cars, and trains. I miss mountains and caverns, archipelagos, capes, and coves. I crave orthodox cathedrals topped with onion turrets and Buddhist temples tucked in bamboo forests. But having set aside my old ideas of cities, and having toured some of the world's finest urban centers, I know that I can live in any city by inhabiting its lore. When I fall asleep to the whir of traffic, wake to sirens or whispers, stroll the rain-damp avenues of my miniature Paris or Athens, I am held tight by the city I have chosen. I live rich with all my myths of Indiana.

Hidden in Plain Sight

TONIGHT, A NIGHT in February, the temperature is expected to fall below zero. This is proving to be one of the hardest winters on record; the city's been overmatched by nature. Snow lies deep on the ground. The street in front of my house has never been plowed; at night when I walk my dog we pick our way over the rough and frozen surface, which catches moonlight like a field of rock crystal.

Winters always seem to take Indianapolis by surprise. If more than an inch or two of snow falls, people seem to freeze behind the wheels of their cars. The city relies on God to clear the side streets. Heaven forbid that any of us should chip in an extra nickel a year to keep our secondary roads clear. Why should we when we know that, eventually, whatever is on the ground will melt?

Here, in a nutshell, is Indiana's yin and yang. That part of us willing to pull the blankets up until the sun shines versus the part that's cursing because packed ice took the muffler off the bottom of our car on the way to that job we know we're lucky to have.

People say Indiana is a conservative state; I don't think that's true. This is actually a reactionary place. Things aren't thought through in an ideological or philosophical way. Public policy here seems based more on fatalism than anything else. Since its founding in the early nineteenth century, Indiana has been run like a kind of colony. The state was once covered with trees, which were chopped down and shipped off to provide hardwood floors for mansions in big cities like Chicago.

Corn was planted where the trees once grew. It, too, was shipped out. Early in the twentieth century, a large part of the state's duneland coast was called "wasteland" and turned into the city of Gary, a relatively temporary structure it turned out, that, for a time, was the industrial center of the world, producing enormous amounts of steel—also exported.

It's hard not to think that, through the years, Indiana has served America better than we have served ourselves. Our agricultural and industrial products have fueled the nation's economy, but, strangely enough, widespread prosperity has somehow eluded us. What with our steel, our crops, and, yes, our Lilly pharmaceuticals, Indiana has arguably had more going for it than many middle-sized nations. Were we to secede from the United States and rely on our own devices, we might think more responsibly about ourselves and where we live.

Until the late 1970s, a kid growing up in Indiana was encouraged to drop out of school as soon as he could to go work on the farm or in a steel mill: to make some real money. Today you see the consequences of this in towns all over Indiana. Communities that relied on family farming or big steel—and whose schools were known only for their basketball teams—look busted at the seams. Colonized by national media—satellite dishes tilting from rooftops like monocultural flags—and abandoned by anyone with so much as a shred of hope for themselves, these places seem out of time, not timeless.

Indiana has a wealth of stories, but little history that anyone can use to build a sense of place that matters. You have to wonder how so much has come to be expunged. Woodland Indian lore, the lives and deaths of the immigrant Irish who built our canals, Eugene Debs's fight for economic justice, the state's virtual takeover by the Ku Klux Klan in the 1920s: scholars have published books on these people and events, but their subjects have little or no hold on the popular imagination. Absent a tradition that honors the love of learning, it's hard to see how this will ever change.

Indiana has paid a heavy price for living in a continual present. Parents are forever telling their children about places, sights, and ways of doing things that no longer exist. History like this is an abstraction. A press release from Indianapolis's recently formed Cultural Development Commission encourages people to visit the new downtown Canal Walk, adding that the Walk is near what *was once* an African American neighborhood with a rich history of jazz. That neighborhood was seized and destroyed by the city in order to build an interstate highway and a commuter campus for Indiana and Purdue universities, which houses the POLIS Center, a think tank devoted to the study of urban life.

My son, Graham, is eighteen years old. Next fall, he'll be going to college in either New York City or Chicago—he'll be leaving Indiana, in other words, and living somewhere else for the first time in his life. This makes Graham part of what, in Indiana, we call "the brain drain"—the trend in our state for young people to come of age and, given the opportunity, move away to some other place.

* * * *

Indiana is America hidden in plain sight. What we need to ask ourselves is why we are so inclined to look at a landscape with soil so rich and harvests so abundant and find it boring. Everyone responds to purple mountains' majesty and oceans white with foam, but put us in a car on Indiana's Highway 421, traversing fields of nutritious green, and our tendency is to turn the radio up and step on the accelerator. Yielding and vulnerable, Indiana's landscape is a pragmatist's dream, a place easily bent to the will of anyone with an axe or a bulldozer. The state was settled by Christians who believed the Lord gave them dominion over the beasts and the fields. This amounted to a kind of license to cut, clear, and dump.

Yet there are rewards for those willing to take the time to stop and look, to pay attention rather than demand sensation. The place encourages a kind of midwestern Zen. The changing seasons, the quality of the light in late afternoon, the presence of wildflowers blooming impetuously in city yards—such pleasures we have in abundance. They don't, unfortunately, qualify as tourist attractions. To our leaders' dismay, Indiana is, undeniably, a backwater. Indianapolis may be one of the largest cities in the United States, but it doesn't even rate a marker on national weather maps. We have to see what's happening in Chicago and Cincinnati and plot what our temperature might be. People are endlessly worrying over what it will take to change this situation. What they fail to realize is that this place only reveals its secrets to those who give up trying to make it seem like anywhere else.

No sooner was Indianapolis settled than people fled its urban center, which was no more than a mile square—a designation defining our downtown that holds to this day. Unlike most other American cities, where people initially lived above the places where they worked, creating densely vertical urban grids, in Indy people almost immediately claimed lots for themselves and proceeded to build single-family dwellings. The city developed in a spacious, residential way. Even its most dilapidated neighborhoods remain collections of houses.

Yin and yang again: we keep to ourselves but are gathered by neighbor-hood. In many ways I am more a citizen of my neighborhood, Broad Ripple, than of the "city" of Indianapolis. The same might be said of folks in nearby Rocky Ripple, or Fountain Square, Butler Tarkington, Chatham Arch, or Williams Creek. You could say, after Thoreau, that we tend to be explorers who stay at home. Most of us recognize the importance of reaching out, the inevitability of globalism. But, at heart, those of us who choose to stay here do so probably in part because some part of us feels the need for a smaller scale. Time and space may be constantly expanding, the nature of consciousness may be infinite, but in order to truly appreciate this, some of us need an offsetting grip on the local. This is possible here.

* * * *

I came to Indiana twenty-some years ago from the San Francisco Bay Area. I was chasing a job at the time and exhausted by the constant struggle to make ends meet in one of the most expensive regions in the country. I remember feeling some trepidation about coming to what I believed was the heart of hard-working America, a place where the work ethic was demanding and unques-tioned. I was surprised and more than a little relieved to discover that, in fact, the place I had come to represented a different story.

San Francisco, supposedly capital of some New Age, was actually a rat race, a place where one competed endlessly for shelter, employment and, most of all, status. In short, rather than subverting traditional American values, life on the coast exemplified them. The Bay Area was not an alternative to American Empire; it was its cutting edge. I wanted out, a kind of exile from all that.

The place I moved to was all but unhanded by the postindustrial economy. Indiana was so far behind the rest of the country people seemed uninterested in even trying to keep up. Work was unhurried—few jobs couldn't be put off until tomorrow. This suited me just fine. Even better was a willingness—more lacka-daisical, I think, than ambitious—on the part of local institutions to give almost anyone with a new idea a chance to try it out, so long as it didn't cost much. I liked this, too. The creative opportunities this admittedly depressed culture was willing to entertain were tremendous. In my time here I've been the state's librarian of the year, produced large-scale urban cultural events, helped create advertising campaigns and made a living through journalism, participated in performance-art projects, and started a public access television station. It's hard for me to imagine casting this wide a net anywhere else—and I'm grateful.

I'm also grateful for the friends I've made, many of whom are artists. Indiana is hardly a destination for the so-called creative class. But it's rich with writers, painters, performing artists, and original thinkers who defy description by discipline. They also defy generalization in terms of movement or style, but I think they share a certain attitude. The artists I know have a hard time fitting in to anyone else's idea of marketplace. That's not to say they don't sell their work or perform it in front of significant audiences, because they do. Nor should one infer that they are without frustration at the lack of a sufficient economy for their works, or that they aren't haunted by doubts about whether this is really the right place to be. Artists here think a lot about fate. Deep bonds are formed; there's a sense of mission. I've learned about community thanks to these people.

My son's grown up among them. When I'm asked to describe the arts scene here, I often find myself telling about how, from the time Graham could walk, his mother and I brought him to the galleries and theaters that engaged us—and to the get-togethers with kindred spirits and collaborators that often followed. Not only was our son accepted in these decidedly adult situations, he was welcomed, spoken to without condescension, his thoughts solicited. We could be artists here without sacrificing our parenthood. Although we may never know how much of this was thanks to the limited career opportunities available, it has always seemed a fair trade.

During the time when our son was in middle school, my wife, Melli, operated a space for experimental dance and theater in the gymnasium of an old Catholic girls' school in downtown Indianapolis. It was a wonderfully funky space, with slightly warped hardwood floors and a towering ceiling complete with slightly askew hanging light fixtures perforated with little crosses. The Susurrus Space, as it was known, drew a modest but wonderfully warm and loyal crowd of artists from around the city, particularly on those annual nights when we held rent parties.

Rent parties gathered dancers, actors, writers, and musicians for an evening of ramshackle inspiration. Somehow they managed to bridge seriousness and fun; the work presented was often astonishing—in part, I suppose because of the casual, throwaway quality with which it was usually presented. There might be a storytelling blues harmonica player for openers, followed by some sci-fi theater, a multimedia dance performance, a poet, and a funk band. A local bartender set up temporary shop in the back, the best vegetarian chef in town provided finger food, and the floor would be filled with tables and folding chairs. On rent party nights, the Space became a magical combination of night-club and living room.

More than the rent party performances, though, I remember what would happen at closing time. Everyone there was asked to help clean the place. Sud-denly the lights came up; people got a little unsteadily to their feet. I can't recall anybody really being in charge. All I know is that in a matter of moments the crowd transformed itself from spectators being entertained to performers of a kind. The party didn't end; it morphed into another dimension. Men, women, kids—everybody was breaking down tables and chairs, moving quickly, asking where things went, working up a sweat. The place was clear in no time. We stepped out into the cold clear night, the city's illuminated skyline rising up over our heads, feeling like we'd just made a little history of our own.

The Susurrus Space is closed now, given over to an office of architects who had the money to renovate it. That is one definition of progress. I suspect, though, that when it comes to creating the kind of community capable of hold-ing young people like my son, our rent parties provide a model that's just as compelling. Ironically, Graham is leaving his hometown to find some place where he can get a larger helping of what we tasted in those days. All blessings on his journey. For the rest of us: the lights are on; there's a lot of cleaning up to do.

Heartland Gentry

Courtesy of the estate of Glenn Watson

"The farmers therefore are the founders of human civilization."

DANIEL WEBSTER

Cider Day

FALL APPROACHES, and the apples fall.

Late-summer apples, green and dewy, scattered over this southern Indiana lawn, like remnants of a neglected game of marbles.

Overhead, a rustle of branches and then the thuds of even more limb-lost apples set the Tell City morning in motion, albeit a lazy sort of motion, the slow stubborn motion of this small town with a city name, the slow, patient motion of the old bones of grandparents gathering fallen apples.

It is mid-September, and it is cider day.

With pocket knives and paring knives, my grandparents carve out small flaws from the fruit's freckled flesh—rot spots, bruises, worm holes—robbing the ripe apples of their roundness, nicked blades dripping with juice, fingers wet and sticky from this seasonal knife-blade geometry.

It is Saturday, and my grandfather rolls out the cider mill and parks it in an apple tree's jagged island of shade. He is one of those retired, toothpick men, a trademark sliver of wood dancing between his lips to some old song playing only in memory, perhaps his favorite song, "I'm the Man That Rode the Mule 'Round The World." This is the same man who, during his prime, labored over Landing Ship Tanks (LSTs) at the Evansville Shipyard as part of the war effort, and after that, led a tool and die maker's long, peaceful life at General Electric.

But now, there are only these apples with which to deal and a leisurely kind of labor.

This cider mill, a muscle-driven machine from another time, was found midpoint last century, buried in some Hoosier man's yard, the wooden hopper and top portion of the flywheel visible above the earth's surface, sprouting from soil like a cast-iron seedling. White letters are etched on the mill: "LATEST IMPROVED BUCKEYE. P.P. Mast and Company. Springfield O." It was built in the 1800s. Time has paled the mill's red paint.

My grandfather dumps the first bowl of apples into the hopper. He turns the handle with his right hand, his left hand hovering to catch any apples that may hop out. Immediately, there's that glorious crunch of apple as the rolling blades in the hopper's base cut the stems, the peels, the cores, the apples' meat, and suddenly I'm gone again, a kid again, in this sweet, apple-scented Saturday morning.

It is a time machine, this cider mill, and I'm taken again to twenty years ago, waiting anxiously behind my barefoot cousins, Tim and Wig and Donald, to turn the handle, keeping a wary eye on the assemblage of buckets and bowls of apples as they are emptied one by one at alarming speed.

Each cousin takes his turn, each effortlessly manhandling the handle in front of our muscular, smiling grandfather. My town-boy-tough cousins are far bigger and stronger than me, the scrawny, rural-route boy of the bunch. As much as I hope that we won't run out of apples before my turn, I also hope we *will* run out of apples. The handle is hard to handle for the small and self-conscious, especially when it assumes the 12 o'clock position, forcing me to stand tiptoed and uncertain.

We never ran out of apples before my turn, though.

By my grandfather's design, I now suspect.

At the cider mill, I am eight, tiptoed and trembling. I hold my breath. I reach up with both hands to clutch the handle, feel the ghost warmth of my cousins' palms, and muster the courage to turn the curvy, cast-iron wheel round and round, faster and faster, silently praying that my hands don't slip and cause the suddenly free-spinning handle to deliver a fearsome upper cut to my jaw, hurtling me into the treetops.

Amazingly, I failed to fail at the cider mill.

The applause of cousins and crunch of apples assure me of this as I close my eyes and turn the humming wheel quite easily with my newfound confidence and strength, feeling my arm muscles tightening, feeling my body moving up and down and round and round until that juice-making machine and I are one.

At eight years old, I became that cider mill.

Though I'm twenty-eight now, and it's just the two of us, I still keep a wary eye on the buckets and bowls of apples. Are we to the last bucket, I ask my grandfather, anxious for my turn after so many years away from the cider mill.

Soon, he says.

After the apple pieces fall into the wooden basket below, the basket is slid forward on a tin runway to the front of the cider mill. Round boards are placed on top of the pile of apple pieces, and when my grandfather turns the thick oily screw that controls the press, the boards are forced downward, pressing the apples tightly until squeezed of their juice. The cider flows forward and drains out the lip of the runway golden and foaming as it is sifted through the sieve of the pan resting in the grass. Hornets and honeybees skim the stream of cider and bounce drunkenly, like bingo balls in a caller's machine.

My grandfather carries the sloshing cider pan into the house and returns with another bucket of apples. It's the last bucket, he tells me, and he dumps the day's last apples into the hopper.

My hand is on the handle, and I turn the wheel, and I hear the crunch, and I see his toothpick smile, and I'm so caught up in cider day here in this Ohio River town, a mere map speck midpoint between our boot-shaped state's tattered toe and crumbled heel, so lost again in the rapture of southern Indiana gravity.

A Country Walk

IT BEGINS AT the northern border of Grant County, at the edge of a field of parched corn struggling from the earth in this hottest and driest of summers.

To the left is a water-starved soybean field; to the right, a modest mobile home, a child's swing, a pickup truck, and an older-model car of indeterminate make. Straight ahead: Grant County Road 500 East, an asphalt strip that weaves and undulates from north to south across the ancient glacial moraine of northeastern Grant County in north central Indiana.

Behind, to the north, is Huntington County. But for a rusted road sign at the intersection, the road ahead is indistinguishable from the road behind, identified in Huntington County as County Road 700 West. In a rare and logical peculiarity of Indiana topography, these rural roads have been assigned numbers corresponding to their distance from the county courthouse. So, on this early summer evening, we are at the junction of Grant County roads 500 East and 700 North, placing us more or less precisely five miles east and seven miles north of the courthouse square in Marion, the county seat of this 418-square-mile chunk of Indiana carved out in 1831. The town—Marion—is named for Francis Marion, the fabled Swamp Fox of Revolutionary War fame; the county—Grant—is named for brothers Samuel and Moses Grant, a pair of Kentuckians slain while fighting Indians in 1789 in present-day Switzerland County.

The mission here is not exploration, but rather idle observation while in the company of a friend marching under orders from his cardiologist. Two miles a day, the doctor has ordered. To alleviate the boredom of the neighborhood closer to home, we have found County Road 500 East, to be examined in one-mile increments (park the car in a farmstead driveway, pacify the ever-present dogs, walk a mile out and a mile back each evening. It will take the better part of a month).

And so we walk the road as it descends, ever so gently, into the valley of the Mississinewa River, crossing Walnut Creek and Lugar Creek and Hummel Creek and a dozen drainage ditches. Past and present are never far removed from one another here. The Lugar pioneers who imposed their name on the stream that flows through Center Township are the stock from which came the senior United States Senator from Indiana, the Hon. Richard Lugar, the diplomatic architect who urged the dismantling of the nuclear arsenal of the former Soviet Union. A very long way from the acreage and sycamores along Lugar Creek.

The asphalt strip passes beneath two high-voltage long-distance power lines and over four Panhandle Eastern Gas Company transmission lines wending their way northeast from the natural gas domes of Texas and Louisiana.

It passes 172 homes; 3 churches; 2 cemeteries; 3 railroad crossings; an abandoned and decaying country school; 1 Pepsi machine and 1 Coke machine, both outside Webster's Market in Fowlerton.

Grant County Road 500 East is a single strip in the latticework of 1,259 miles of streets and roads that crisscross Grant County. It runs exactly 20.8 miles from the Huntington County line to the triangular junction of Grant, Madison, and Delaware counties to the south. The county is 19 miles across; the additional 1.8 miles is the accumulated distance of jogs and doglegs in the road between the two ends. Some deviations from straight accommodate terrain. Others are, no doubt, the result of political dealing: a four-hundred-foot jog in Fairmount Township leaves a section of good tillable land unbisected and, not incidentally, takes the road down the broad main drag of the town of Fowlerton. In 1831, the businessmen of Fowlerton had grand plans. One can conjure the discussion:

"The county road will miss us."

"Not if we get them to move the road. I can speak with the county commissioners about that."

Along these 20.8 miles is spread a panorama of life in rural Indiana, a tableau of history in Washington, Center, Mill, and Fairmount townships, punctuated here and there by the evidence of day-to-day life: washed clothing drying in the summer breeze; dogs trained to bark menacingly at approaching strangers; suntanned children riding bicycles; gardeners picking and scratching at the dry earth, robbed by drought this summer of much of its greenery. A portrait of the commonplace fashioned in four of Indiana's 1,016 townships.

Except for Fowlerton and the intersection on the map that is Hanfield, Grant County Road 500 East avoids contact with towns, preferring to amble across land dedicated to the production of corn, soybeans, silage, feeder cattle, dairy herds, firewood, and winter wheat.

But despite its best effort to shun settlements, it has failed. Along the road, scattered here and there, subdivisions have taken root. The majority of the 172 homes along the way are new homes, one-story houses with multicar garages, basketball courts in the driveways, and the now-familiar television satellite dishes aimed from the rooftops and backyards toward a satellite 22,000 miles away in the southwest sky. Those who frequent rural America, away from the umbilical cord of cable television, will tell you that it is impossible now to lose your way. The satellite dish, they assure you, is invariably focused on the southwest sky. Find a satellite dish and you can reckon your direction.

There are, certainly, some of the fine old midwestern farm homes: solid, rambling, two-story white-frame structures with large front porches, plenty of rooms and windows, and a full complement of surrounding outbuildings. But they are fewer than they once were. Such a home near County Road 700 South on County Road 500 East now shelters only the spirit of the farm family past. The windows are shattered, and the paintless siding is bleached to a dull gray. The farms are larger, the farmsteads fewer.

To walk, one step at a time, across the expanse of Grant County is to sample the life of the land, past and present.

It is to encounter seven-year-old David Dyer and his dog Sparky, sitting in front of the Dyer home at 1000 South and 500 East.

It is to encounter eighty-five-year-old Alvin Ford on the swing at his home on the main street of Fowlerton and listen to him talk about how Fowlerton became Fowlerton:

"When I came here in 1904, they had just changed the name from Leachburg to Fowler. But that still didn't suit 'em, so they tacked on a little more and called it Fowlerton."

It is to stand on the shore of Lake Galatia, a remnant of the Ice Age, and consider the day back in 1904 when men working on Dora Gift's farm dug up the bones of a giant mammoth that had become mired in the muck near the lake and died fifteen or twenty thousand years ago. The much-heralded skeleton stands today on a pedestal in the Museum of Natural History in New York City.

And it is to walk quietly among the weathered stones of the 130-year-old Fletcher Chapel Church graveyard at 200 North and 500 East. Enoch and Sarah Cranston are buried here.

Enoch was born in 1836 and died in 1897. His wife lived another seven years, long enough to see in the twentieth century. Beside them rests James Dillon, who died in 1872 and was buried here inside the wrought iron fence that defines the graveyard. He was fifty-four years, five months, and seven days old. Young Albert Bowman is buried here beneath a weathered white stone. He was only fifteen years old when he died in 1905. And Amy Counts. She was born in 1818—just six years after the War of 1812's Battle of the Mississinewa was fought ten miles west of here. The Fletcher Chapel graveyard has been her resting place for 120 years now.

This road, this elongated neighborhood, is home to the McIntyre family and the Klinger family, and the Blakes and the Atkinsons and Sprinkles and Disneys and Henrys and so many others.

It is home to eleven-year-old Aaron Peters, who lives with his parents, Mark and Mary Peters, at 150 North and 500 East. Aaron wears a Chicago Bears T-shirt and rides a motorcycle with heavy-duty deep-tread tires.

To the south of the Peters' home is the Pulley family home place, a two-story brick home that has stood here for better than a century. Two world wars and everything else that has happened away from County Road 500 East have not fazed it. Adam Pulley, William B. Pulley, William M. Pulley, Samuel Pulley, and Jane Pulley each owned parcels of land here in Washington Township a century ago. Some of the land is still in the stewardship of Pulley descendants.

On down the road, near County Road 500 East's intersection with County Road 100 North, is a manicured home and lawn with a sign boasting that this is the home and headquarters of Carol's Cakes and Catering.

Back up the road, at Hanfield, a car full of young people comes to a stop in a screech of tires and a cloud of dust. These are Hanfield's teenagers: Jason Holm, John and Jeff Walters, Tom Purtee, and Kim Pickard. Blue jeans, gym shoes with untied laces, and longish hair are the fashion among Hanfield's youth. Despite their menacing arrival, they are pleasant and conversational. Their common goal, they agree, is to live someplace other than Hanfield, Indiana.

"When I graduate, you're gonna see a diploma and dust," one says. The others agree. County Road 500 East in the rearview mirror.

There are other traits common to the inhabitants along County Road 500 East:

American flags. They flutter in the breeze from poles imbedded in concrete in lawns. They hang gracefully from porch overhangs. Some are small. Others large. One is paired with the blue field of the state flag of Indiana.

Dogs. Minimum requirement at each of the 172 residences, it seems, is at least one. Many have two. One home near the Wheeling Pike intersection boasts at least a half dozen. All bark with authority, though some wag tails in a friendlier gesture.

And land. It is always the land that dominates. Frank Hix, a young farmer who is worried about the fate of his soybean crop this year, has a family name that dates back to 1831 in this area. In the 1877 Atlas of Grant County is an account of James Hix and his land.

On the farm of James Hix, about 1840, an old-fashioned Methodist Camp Meeting was held. This farm for a number of years was used as a place for such meetings. Doubtless there are many who regard this almost as holy ground, remembering that is was here "they put off the old man" by humbling themselves at the foot of the cross and pleading for God's mercy.

Frank Hix, thirty-three, who with his father, Ben, seventy-two, is a grain and dairy farmer, sits atop his tractor on the asphalt roadway in late evening surveying the expanse of land he cultivates. He speaks of drought and proper planting and how proper discing of the soil and placement of the seeds at the proper depth may make a big difference come harvest. In the distance, his dairy herd begins to approach the barbed wire fence along County Road 500 East, led by a bull of questionable temper.

"He's just curious. He makes a lot of noise, but he's really good natured," Hix says as he positions his cultivator between the rows of soybeans and begins the task of keeping the aisles clear of weeds.

The land. Along the 20.8 miles most of the land is open. The homes and lawns and barns and outbuildings occupy very little of the land. Most is in corn and soybeans. Patches here and there are planted in winter wheat, now beginning to turn golden. There is an occasional oat field and some pastureland and a few good wood lots. But most of the land is cleared and open without interruption to the horizon.

And in the soft light of the setting sun, one thinks of the task of clearing this land a century-and-a-half ago. When the white man came and claimed the land from the Indian—stole it, some would suggest—this was timberland, the far edge of the great forest that extended west from the Atlantic Ocean across the Appalachians to the valley of the Wabash. An agile squirrel, so it was claimed, could travel from the great ocean to the Great Lakes without ever touching the ground. Limb to limb, tree to tree, forest to forest.

Along County Road 500 East is a rare example of what the land was like before it was subdued by the settlers. It is Botany Glen, a forty-acre preserve and living laboratory at 500 East and the Wheeling Pike intersection. It is owned by Indiana Wesleyan University in Marion. It is a tangle of brush and foliage, punctured here and there by great, towering oaks, sycamores, walnut, and maple trees. Somewhere in there is the foundation of a farmhouse, but as the land has reverted to its natural state, it has all but erased any evidence of settlement.

Look at the timber and foliage and consider this: The languages of the Eastern Woodland Indians had no word meaning "wilderness" as it is understood in English. All was wilderness and none was wilderness. It was as it was, and it was home to plants and animals and man alike.

A half mile north of Botany Glen is the Mississinewa River, the artery that brought the people and their possessions to this land. Rising in Darke County, Ohio, the Mississinewa meanders through east central Indiana on its journey to the larger Wabash east of Peru.

"It is, as rivers go, a fairly young river, a little more than 15,000 years old," historian Richard Simons wrote of the Mississinewa. Along this river a dozen miles to the northwest, Goldsmith Gilbert, the first white man in this land, set up a post to trade with the Miami Indians in 1823. His boatload of trade goods came down this river, floated past this point where County Road 500 East now spans the stream.

And before him, in 1808, Tecumseh's brother, the one-eyed, ill-tempered, self-styled Prophet of the Shawnee nation, Tenskwatawa, led a flotilla of canoes past this spot as he took his disciples from Greenville, Ohio, to their new village at Prophetstown, where the bloody Battle of Tippecanoe would be fought three years later.

On this June evening birds and bats dart and swoop back and forth across the stream from trees on one bank to trees on the opposite bank. A duck floats leisurely downstream past a load of dumped trash—including the hulk of a rusted refrigerator, a jolting and disgusting reminder of man's intrusion. Here, at this spot where the Mason Bridge carries County Road 500 East over the river, the past and the present are very close indeed.

The bridge walls, which have stood since 1937, are a gallery of graffiti recording the romances of the young people of the neighborhood: "Shane M. & Brian R." have left their crude autographs. And there is this announcement in Day-Glow orange: "Denny Smith loves Shannon Decker."

Throughout the journey are encounters with people. Pleasant encounters.

Back up the road, up near the traffic zipping back and forth on the four lanes of Indiana 18, a jogger explains his determination: "The sign says the speed limit is 25 miles an hour." Robert Breedlove and his daughters Patty and Lisa are bicycling at a saner pace and pause to take a look at the trickle of water in Lugar Creek. Bobby Bandy and Billy Rice are riding in a wagon pulled by a garden tractor. The children are going to camp tonight behind the Bandy home and are in search of wood for a campfire. Cousins Sam and John Skeens have propped themselves up against a pickup truck in front of Sam's home across the road from Lake Galatia. They are considering the potential for bass fishing. On this night they will get no closer than talking about it. Pond scum on the surface of the lake is a problem, they agree.

At Fowlerton, Cassie, Brian, Stephanie, Cheri, and Kayla haul a wagon full of soft drink bottles to Webster's Market, exchange the bottles for quarters, plunk the quarters into the Pepsi and Coke machines, and leave with the beginning of a new cache of bottles.

Down the road from Fowlerton on the left is the imposing ninety-nine-year-old skeleton of Fairmount Township District 5 school, empty now as it has been for several decades. What stories these brick walls ought to tell before they crumble. But, of course, they won't.

In the last mile between the skeletal school and the county line there used to be a tile factory. But it's gone, has been for years. Nothing now along these final few thousand feet of County Road 500 East but some fields of scrawny corn, which will yield little this fall.

What is remarkable about this journey is how unremarkable it is. It lives only in its specificity: the places and names and faces along this road. It is merely an asphalt thread, a single strand woven into the web of roads across the ninety-two counties of Indiana. The road, County Road 500 East, is only an incision that arbitrarily divides parcels of property and pockets of people. Life along County Road 600 East or 400 West or any other road we might travel would be identical in all but the details. It is, finally, that which makes it remarkable. It is a 20.8-mile journey into all that is Indiana. That is remarkable.

Country Roads Lined with Running Fences: A Dozen Story Problems about the Place of Place

1

WHERE TO HAVE LUNCH? One summer, in Centerville, Iowa, I had supper in a restaurant on the largest town square in the world. At one time, chances were good that on most town squares of the Midwest there would be a steak place, a pizza parlor, a soda fountain, or a newsstand run by a Greek family. Perhaps the only indication was a special salad on the menu, a gyros machine by the grill, or a fading picture of a white island and blue water tacked to the wall. Ten years before, George, the restaurant owner, came to Centerville from the Peloponnese by the way of the Quad Cities, where he had family in the restaurant business. He worked most of the year but shut down for a season to return to Greece with his family. He told me he has sent his wife and child back for good now since he wants the boy to grow up there. One day, he thinks, he'll return for good. It is the winter he has never grown used to. Though Centerville has been very good for business, it can never be home. When I told him how much I've liked traveling in Greece, how I look to make it over there again, he did something remarkable. He scribbled down his name and the addresses of cousins in Athens, folks in his village, and told me where to find them when I am in Kalamata. "Ask for Yiorgos," he said. "Say that you are from Iowa."

2

Iowa is where exactly? Actually, I am from Indiana—that's where I was born and grew up. I know the feel of the Midwest. In Ireland, in Poland, in Italy one can sense a loss and a resignation to the fact that much of the country's population lives somewhere else. America as a nation has never suffered a diaspora, but natives of Iowa, of Indiana, and of the Midwest know of this fate. Our migrations are internal, our shifts of population covered by an easy freedom to move about and an illusion that most places are the same or can be made to feel the same. Talking with George in Centerville, Iowa, reminded me of Greece, where most everyone has a friend or relative who has gone away. And being reminded of that brought me home, back to Iowa, to Indiana, to my midwestern home, where people have not gone to a new country, but they have certainly gone away.

3

Where exactly is this Midwest? Where are its borders? What are its colors on the map? It depends on whom you ask. Iowans generally sketch roughly the Big Twelve Athletic Conference states—Iowa, Nebraska, Kansas, Missouri, and the Dakotas—as the prime midwestern states. Sometimes they will reach for Oklahoma and Colorado. When asked about Indiana or Ohio the usual consensus is that those places lie in the East. They are surprised to learn that Hoosiers think of the Midwest as the Big Ten Conference—Michigan, Ohio, Indiana, Illinois, Minnesota, Wisconsin, and part of Iowa. Iowans want to know what "Easterners" from Indiana would call what they call the Midwest. I say the plains, of course. It becomes more interesting when I ask what defines a midwestern state. It must be rooted in agriculture, they say. I answer that it should be a balance between farming and manufacturing. They narrow their definition. The agriculture must be a special kind. It must be corn. Their definition of the Midwest derives from their home state, of course. It hasn't defined anything at all, but has been shaped to fit the place.

4

Where exactly is the Midwest? We should perhaps be more interested in what the confusion reveals than in pinning down the actual boundaries of the place, though it is probably wise to spend a few moments in definition. Again, where is the Midwest? And beyond that, what does characterize the region? How does it differ from other regions? Does it differ at all? These are important questions in developing a sense of place. Perhaps we assign an identity too easily, use the names without thinking what we want them to represent. Despite the confusion about its location, people agree that the Midwest is a good place to be *from*. It is as if we keep the region purposely vague in order to include as many people as possible as natives. "I am *from* the Midwest": that coin is worth collecting.

5

What is the real question? So the real question is why do so many of us want to be from a place that is nowhere and everywhere? The preposition is important, the *from*. Even those of us who still live in the Midwest, no matter how you define it, still would say we are from the Midwest, as if its special properties rub off on us only at birth and that since birth we have been getting further and further away.

6

What is what it is not? Dorothy realizes when she bumps down in Oz that she is not in Kansas anymore. If there is anything that characterizes a literature of the Midwest, it is this sense of discovery through absence. Nick Carraway, the narrator of F. Scott Fitzgerald's *The Great Gatsby*, realizes as the story ends that it is a tale of the Midwest and of a midwesterner in New York totally unequipped to live in the East. As the novel ends, he is preparing to return home. Leaving home, the Midwest, in order to see home clearly is a driving force in the themes of midwestern literature and life. Stories of the Midwest often begin at the moment of turning back from afar and the hero gaining sight for the first time of a distant beauty. Living in the Midwest, we know a truth about this coming and going. Many, many people have left, but few actually return. Though Dorothy keeps demanding to be sent home, though she tells us once she is home that there is nothing like it, we are uneasy. It is a black and white world in Kansas. Why would she, why would we, leave the technicolor of Oz?

7

What does New Jersey have to do with anything? A friend who grew up in New Jersey noticed right away that the Midwest had no walls. There are picket fences, strung wire, cyclone mesh, the red staves of snow fence, chicken wire, barbed wire, even electric line. But no walls. My friend defines the Midwest that way—a country woven in wire fence—and he always argues that beyond the lack of boulders in the ground to build walls, the fences reflect something else inherent in the people who live here. You can see through fences, he says. They do not block out the subtle and endless beauty of the prairie and field. But at the same time the fence breaks up that vast and overwhelming horizon into bits of manageable places. The fence builders want it both ways. It is an aesthetic compromise between private property and being part of a neighborhood. A fence allows its builder to say, "I am alone. Separate, not different. I've got nothing to hide, but don't come too close." It is a delicate balance. There are many

such balances here between the individual and the community. The fences of
the Midwest give us tangible evidence of the web of these relationships.

8

**What does the current disappearance of fences and fencerows tell us about the
state of affairs now?** The disappearance of fencerows could be written off to the
use of larger machines with broader turning radii, the lack of animals on farms,
the trouble of maintaining the wire. But does it reveal something deeper? The
simplest definition of place carries within it the notion of limits, of boundary.
Part of what we believe as Americans, indeed what brought many people here in
the first place, includes the contradictory idea of a country unbounded, a place
of limitless opportunity. In the realm of advertising's easy diction, *you can have
it all.* The disappearance of physical fences in the midwestern landscape might
represent a transformation, a shift in interior space as well. A rickety, rusty wire
fence was the product of the meeting between the irresistible force of individual
enterprise and the immovable object of community. Fences snare and enmesh
but are flexible, movable, many gated. Their disappearance could signal to us the
release of an unbridled force that is dangerous to community. An article in the
Des Moines Register on the obsolescence of the township included a picture showing the entire government and voting body of a township in Iowa: a farmer, his
wife, and their daughter. The question that arises is this: When does a town stop
being a town? What is the critical mass of a community? The presence of fences
tells us finally that there are people here, that the land is divided up among them.
As people have left the Midwest, the fences have come down. Their absence does
not bring people closer together but only indicates that there is no one here.
Someone will always own the land, but someone will not always live here.

9

Where did they go? The roads that have taken people away can also be thought
of in the same way as fences—as physical manifestations of our interior feelings
about place and the land. As we've seen, they are the quickest way out of town
for our writers, our children, our friends, ourselves, but are also the way back.
Roads, too, form our boundaries. The section roads lie like a net over the land,
divide it, define it, parcel it out, and impose the order of place. But the road is
also a common way owned by no one and everyone. When we think usually of
the literature of the road, say of Jack Kerouac, we think of the road as a con-
veyor, as something that moves through, something that is part of somewhere

else. Yet it is also part of the things that stay put. We treat the road as Euclideans would have us treat a line—the distance between two points having no width. But the road, the sidewalk, the corners, the squares are rich with metaphoric meanings where once again the individual meets the group of which he or she is a part. The road may bound us, but it also binds us together. The road is a place itself, as a fencerow is, and both must be thought of more as transmitting membranes, like skin, at once tough and intimate.

10

Can you be more specific? Good writing is always specific. Henry James wrote that good writing is "selected perception and amplification." There is literally a world of difference between using one word over another, "a" instead of "the." As a writer selects words, he or she is making a series of choices that include or exclude parts of the world. William Faulkner called the county in Mississippi he wrote about his "postage stamp of land." Though writers narrow and select, they often cordon off a precinct sacred to them. Readers discover that within those boundaries there are areas of human experience that seem unlimited. Perhaps it is a quirk in the way we are made, but it appears the more specific a writer is, the easier it is for a reader to generalize. In geometry, we know that a finite plane bounded on all sides still contains infinite points. Stories, poems, and essays work that way, too. The more tightly bounded, the more restricted a work is, the richer we find it. Author and authority are related words. To be author of a specific place is, in a way, to be its god, its creator. But the place a god creates can never be as detailed as the larger world it is part of, for the writer faces the fact that he or she is limited, mortal. Writing then, by its limitation, by acknowledging its human scale, still participates in something grand. The writer shares in the creation of the universe by creating a postage stamp. In Thorton Wilder's *Our Town,* a character receives a letter addressed to her, her street, her town, her state, her country, her planet, her solar system, and on until it ends with the mind of God. Her thrilled response is that it got *here* anyway. It got here.

11

Can you tell us a story? If books are like places, then places are like books. Let me tell you a story. I was helping a farmer during planting. I was driving a tractor, vibrashanking a field of soybean stubble as the farmer followed behind me planting corn. The operation I was asked to do was an easy one, but I don't have much aptitude for machines. I wound up during one pass almost sliding into a

ditch of water when I tried to make the turn. Braking, I stalled the engine, and
shaken, I couldn't get the thing in gear to start up again. The farmer all this
time was steadily catching up. The harder I tried to free myself and prove my
competence, the worse things got. The farmer's son was working in the next
field. He yelled to me that he was on his way to help. In a few minutes I saw him
poling down the ditch on a raft made of old fence posts, and he saved the day.
There isn't much to the story. That's not why I told it. What is interesting is that
when I visit that farm now, sooner or later that little story is told again—how
Michael got stuck and Eric came to the rescue. Sometimes it is told to people
who haven't heard the story. But more often than not, we tell it to ourselves. It
is as if the story is another building constructed a few springs ago. It is a part
of the layout of the place, part of the map. This little story takes its place with
hundreds of others. The field where I had my adventure is called Cottonwood
for the tree that used to be there sixty years ago. When Farmer Brown tells Eric
to cultivate Cottonwood, it is a one-word story. The tree no longer exists. The
story does. Places exist in two dimensions. They exist in the physical realm, but
also in time. I will exist as part of a place on that farm as long as people tell
the story. Though the dirt, the ditch, the crops exist, a place needs a person to
name it. Cottonwood. It is interesting what we call the documents that transfer
land: deeds and titles. The land itself carries its own deeds and titles. To gain a
sense of place is to be sensitive to stories about places.

12

Here's your hat; what's your hurry? A sense of place is a complex idea further confounded by our relationship to it. We all labor to resolve two opposing
forces in our lives. On one hand we have a desire to be rooted, to belong—literally to be long—in a place. On the other hand, we wish to be free of those
connections, to keep moving through. As with all compelling conflicts, this one
is not easily resolved, probably not to be resolved. People now move far more
than they stay put. By moving we find it easier to ignore those limits imposed on
our lives. The fences on either side of the road seem more like a chute channel-
ing us on to some wonderful future. To have a sense of place is to sense limits,
to sense our own deaths, a specific plot of ground where we will be buried and
where our bodies will become part of the plot of ground. By accepting the limits
a place imposes, we gain the ability to leave a mark. By being part of a place, we
become it.

Wish You Were Here

IT WAS BURT LANCASTER'S debut as a director and Walter Matthau's debut as an actor, but the few folks in town who would drift over to the Lincoln Pioneer Village would go to see their neighbors as movie extras, not to see the stars.

It was 1955, summer, midweek, midmorning, and Hollywood had come to Rockport, an unexcitable little town that sat with its toes in the Ohio River at the southernmost tip of Indiana. You could spit and hit a Kentuckian, as the locals liked to say when describing the area's geographic location to the occasional stranger, and with the filming of Lancaster's rustic tale in full swing the joke had taken on new meaning; no one possesses a keener sense of sarcasm or irony than a farmer. And Rockport was a typical midwestern farming community's town in the fifties, with just enough architecture and asphalt to differentiate itself from field. Still, the field was where most folks were, or the hardware store or courthouse or wherever they were that had nothing to do with moviemaking but everything to do with their daily routines of work and more work, exactly what my mother and grandfather had been doing since before daylight until we headed into town in the old green truck.

Also, people who live in dry climates don't understand humidity, and how combined with heat it expands exponentially with the advancement of clock and calendar, how insidious its nature. But folks in Spencer County, Indiana, had to make peace with the bully every summer by spending evenings in the porch swing, drinking pitchers of lemonade, sleeping through the turning of the bed pillow every hour or so to find the less sweaty and therefore cooler side.

Only the bank and the funeral parlor were air-conditioned, certainly not the average farmhouse. In an hour or two it would be "right close," and by midafternoon it would be "right close indeed," but midmorning was just the heralding time of day, a heads up if you will, for what was coming.

But the air coming up through the wide floor vent and in the door windows of the old truck was still cool at this hour and speed—approximately forty miles per hour—even for me sandwiched between my mother and grandfather. I tilted my head back, closed my eyes, and let it rush upward along my knobby legs and over my face, ruffling my eyelashes and blowing back my bangs. The two adults talked, slightly louder to lift their voices over road noise and because my grandfather had started to lose his hearing, and the conversation ran its usual course around grain prices and machinery repairs and last night's supper like a pony around a ground tie, mostly my grandfather doing the talking. What they did not talk about was the event they would "swing by" after the Co-Op but before the A & P. The event was a movie being made in our little hometown on a bluff overlooking the Ohio. They hadn't talked about it, though, so I hadn't thought about it. Mostly I was just happy to be along for the ride, maybe a little hopeful for a penny candy at the grocery store if I was very, very good.

I remember my mother braked hard to miss a rabbit that darted across the road just before the red-brick orphanage that sat like a new kid at recess, far off from the highway in a line of scrawny pines. The sudden jerk threw me forward, almost to the broad dashboard, before she grabbed my left arm and yanked me in reverse, my grandfather grabbing at me from the other direction with the crook of his cane. He made jokes about the rabbit stew he could have had for supper, but I could only picture Flopsy, Mopsy, and Cotton Tail in the book I loved at the library. I sat up straight and kept my eyes open the rest of the way, in case another rabbit might try the same dumb thing, venturing too far.

They bought various items at the Farm Bureau Co-Op, but the only one I remember was cotton rope. When the man behind the counter—who called me by name and asked about my pet duck QuackQuack and after my father, who was working at his other full-time job with Ma Bell—when he rolled that white rope into a mess of circles it made me think of the rabbit again, and I was glad to hold the soft loop of it in the truck. I remember their talk turned to humidity, then, while the morning climbed the sky and took the breeze with it like a kite takes its tail, because if you stood still long, or in the sun at all, parts would want to stick to other parts, like a stamp when you don't lick it enough wants to stick to the envelope but can't quite—and we had all stood around in the Farm Bureau just that long.

When my mother turned onto Main Street the new shovel handle rolled side to side in the bed of the truck, and because a farmer's attention always follows the direction of every new sound my grandfather automatically swiveled his head to look. He clicked his false teeth at me and I pretended not to hear him, but I smiled and I knew he saw me. I knew then that the penny candy was a sure thing unless I forgot to say thank you or please or call Mrs. Lincoln at the A & P ma'am when she asked how I was and I said fine, ma'am.

We passed the grocery then, and the funeral parlor, and a one-man barbershop where my grandfather got his mostly bald head shined up once in a while and his face splashed with blue liquid from a tall glass bottle that smelled very bad in my opinion but always made him pleased with himself. He mostly went there before he took the C. & E. I. train over to Peoria, Illinois, where a lady he had known a long time lived. I didn't get to go into town much when the barbershop was one of the stops, because he and my father would be hauling water or feed on those days and there was no room for me, which even then I knew meant no time to fool with a little kid underfoot. The chance of getting penny candy on those days was "slim to none," as my family likes to say when you might as well give up hoping, so I didn't much care about having to stay behind.

When we passed the medical center, a two-doctor establishment and the only new building in town, the one with the glass-block windows and the rows of silver-armed chairs inside, my grandfather made a comment about a horse one of the doctors owned, how it was a biter, how he'd told Doc to bite the animal back. My mother laughed so we all laughed, and then we were turning the slow grade downward at the end of Main Street and snaking back the other way, gradually upward into the city park's dense deciduous shade where the Pioneer Village stood.

I learned years later, probably in high school, that the Lincoln Pioneer Village had been built in the hard times after World War I by the WPA, the Works Progress Administration, a New Deal brainchild of President Franklin D. Roosevelt who knew that to put men back on their feet meant to let them earn a living. But I didn't know about any of that on this day, a bright calm summer day the year I turned four, or that a cabin inside was dedicated to one of my own relatives, Aunt Lepha Mackey, a white woman who took it upon herself to be the first teacher of black children in Spencer County. In fact, before that day I had never been to the Pioneer Village, or even heard of it, or of Lincoln, or of much to do with the world outside our farm, even though I could identify each grain, each stalk or leaf, each type of animal, the sounds of machinery, the poisonous from the nonpoisonous, and all the things farm kids learned from the cradle back then.

My mother pulled into the semicircle lane and parked, and we got out and headed toward the entrance, where tall wooden doors that swung outward were held by leather straps looped over wooden pins in the towering, split-log fence. I thought of the book in the library with the picture of Davy Crockett standing atop a similar fence in his coonskin cap. Here, as in that picture, everything was dark brown, the color of wet tree trunks; everything was wood: the fence, the little cabins I could just glimpse inside, the ax-hewn benches lining the entrance way, the trees thick along the lane, everything dark brown and lovely. And it smelled lovely, too. Like bark and dirt and grass and tree roots and leaves blowing high above your head and clean-sheet clouds beyond that and birds up there somewhere swirling and swooping around between you and the bright giggling yellow sun. *Ahhh* I must have said aloud, or some other vowel-consonant transmission that tells mothers they should take hold of their children's hands, because my mother did that, reached down and took my hand as if to say "remember your manners now, be a good girl," and we walked right up to the entrance where a very few other people from town stood watching, and my mother stepped aside long enough that I could wiggle in front of her for a better look.

There wasn't much to see. From the shady entrance tunnel, it seemed that bright sunshine inside the village bounced up from the yard and flashed against every long white apron or bonnet the movie extras wore. There were women costumed in long skirts, and men in suspenders and big-sleeved shirts and dark pants that didn't cover their boots, "high water britches" my grandfather called them, and children in smaller versions of the same clothes, none seeming too happy about it. Everyone looked hot, a bit impatient, and the kids especially had begun to droop already, like pulled weeds tossed to the garden's edge.

One of the women spied my mother, threw up her big, wiggly arm and waved, grinning broadly as I had seen her do at the grocery or post office, and my mother flashed the inside of her palm in return the way she always did. One flash, up and right back down, quick and to the point, nothing flamboyant like the short round woman in the long hot costume. When folks in my family waved, you had to look at their faces instead of their hands to know how they meant to greet you. The woman milled around briefly inside the bright sun, talking with other extras, fanning her thick neck with her bonnet, and then a man instructed them to take their places again, so they did.

I couldn't see too far left or right, mostly just straight ahead, so I couldn't see the people lined up across the yard from the ones in front of me, but I knew

they all looked alike and that there was some problem among them, some conflict, and that that was what they were pretending about.

It was quiet, I remember, except for a man's voice that carried over the
slowing breeze, telling everyone what to do next. And then I heard a clapping
sound, and they all posed as if they were their own paper dolls, even the children, and then something happened I couldn't see, and then they all stopped
again, and fanned themselves and milled about some more. This happened
two, maybe three times, and then my mother put her hands on my shoulders
and turned us both around to leave. I was just getting the hang of it, just getting
the rhythm of the stopping and starting, and so I wanted to stay to see what happened next, and because my head was still turned for a longer look I saw a man
carry a single black box on three legs into my line of vision and set it down in
the grass, and I knew that was the thing they were all trying to please.

I wanted to go back, tried to tell my mother, but she shushed me and kept
on going, plowing me by the skinny shoulders to the old truck and my waiting
grandfather who had evidently seen enough long before she had, even though
he'd stood so far back from the entrance I couldn't understand how he had
seen anything at all.

As we pulled out, a farm truck loaded with salt licks, Co-Op dog food, a
wheelbarrow, and three dirty boys in the bed pulled in, and my grandfather
lifted the cigar between his fingers at the driver as hello, but over my shoulder I
saw most of the vehicles leaving the semicircle to head back toward Main Street,
the few townsfolk who had meandered over to look finding nothing to look
at except their friends and neighbors standing around in the rising heat and
humidity in silly costumes, doing pretty much nothing.

My grandmother read the local newspaper that week as always, sitting in her
grandpa's rocker after the supper dishes were done up and her apron was on
the hook behind the kitchen door. I sat at the table and sewed old buttons onto
a long string as she read from cover to cover, three whole turns of the yellowish,
ink-smelling paper, and I remember she said something like "an' here you go
now, here's your big trip to town to see the movie bein' made, well idn't that
somethin'," and then she read with real interest the church news about two bap-
tisms and the birth of twins and how unusual that was, two and two in the same
week. The paper ran a picture, of the movie not the church news, and in it was
the man I had seen with the black box on legs. It was an action shot, that's what
my grandmother read aloud, which made her chuckle since my grandfather
had told her right off there was little action going on, that he was glad those

"work brittle" Hollywood folks didn't have to raise the crops since he was pretty sure they'd starve to death, the rest of us with them. In the background of the picture was the big, jiggly-armed woman who had waved at my mother looking fiercely perturbed at an invisible foe. She was a good pretender, I guessed.

And that was the end of it. The movie was made and marketed and met with little success. I read later that Burt Lancaster didn't direct again for two decades after *The Kentuckian.* I remember wondering what my grandmother would have made of that, the number two coming up again, since when Lancaster did return to the back side of the black box it was to direct his second, and last, film, though he acted in dozens and became a major Hollywood star. I don't think he ever came back to Rockport, Indiana, though.

It's funny what you remember, what sticks in your mind as significant. I guess what's funny too is how those memories burrow into your personality and perspective. Even as a kid I knew the tone and rhythm of the place where I lived, the pitch of the folks who lived there with me, and how the outside world, whatever it was, was a different composition of treble and bass. People in the southern tip of Indiana were hard to impress, for one thing. Hollywood had come to them, for pity's sake, but they could have cared less. They had Johnson grass to fight, clothes to hang on the line, pigs to ring, sweet tomato relish to put up, and children to teach manners. Years after the event, I learned in casual conversation that most folks in town had gone about their business as usual during the filming of Lancaster's movie, and the few who bothered to venture into the city park only came to see people they knew, and only after they'd been to Tig's Café for homemade cherry pie. It was as I had remembered it, barely a ripple on the pond of important events, barely even a curiosity.

So a few years later, when my grandmother climbed into my old bachelor uncle's shiny new eggplant-colored Edsel and they headed for the Ozarks, I watched them pull out of the drive and head down the long stretch of gravel road, rolling dust up over the trunk of the car and out across the ditches to blanket the tiger lilies. Then I went back to the barn to finish the stalls, and after that a list of chores as long as a horse's tail, and by then it was late afternoon and I had the porch swing and a thick book to myself. Never did I wonder what they would see or where they'd go; I knew they'd tell us all about it when they got back, and besides home was a good enough place to be, especially in the porch swing with a book.

They did come home, of course, a week or so later, and finally sometime after that a postcard arrived: WISH YOU WERE HERE it said on the front in bold

Adirondack-style letters above a picture of yellow-topped dark green mountains; on the back in fountain pen in my grandmother's careful script was a single line saying how lovely the trees were. I don't know why I kept that postcard. Something about the invitation it offered, I suppose, something about the compare-and-contrast nature of it, the outside world with my world, the outside world with me. Maybe I kept it because it was the beginning of my growing wanderlust; I just don't know. But I kept many postcards in the years to come, some from exotic ports of call another uncle saw compliments of the U.S. Navy, some from hard-earned family vacations, some from pen pals or friends who traveled.

When I was old enough to strike out myself, I bought them at every Stuckey's or mom-and-pop diner or truckstop along the blue highways of America, not to send but to keep. I don't know why I did that either, why I still do. What I do know is that wherever HERE refers to I only think of Indiana, of the flat endless fields of corn and soybeans or the softly ebbing fields of winter wheat or rye, the hay rolls and grain silos and barns full of tractors and livestock, the long driveways to plain white houses with porches with rocking chairs, of dogs that know who's friendly and who's suspect, of basketball and church bazaars and family reunions with homemade ice cream, and trees everywhere, like dark brown crayons, lovely. To describe the Indiana of my childhood almost turns it into cliché, or sentimental drivel. I guess you just had to be here then.

* * * *

In 1969, fourteen years after Burt Lancaster and his crew took Highway 66 out of Rockport never to return, I left home for college on Highway 41 thinking I'd never return either. I had big plans. The world was waiting for me, and I couldn't wait to oblige it. And then one day when I should have been studying but was watching television with friends instead, a program called *Sesame Street* came on. I had never heard of it, or children's television programming for that matter, so I sat fascinated as a parade of letters and numbers and animated characters of every bright hue and texture paraded before me. And then a real man appeared, and I was not just watching with the fascination of a child, I *was* a child again for a split second. It was Burt Lancaster. Unbelievable, I thought to myself, how small the world really is, what continuity there is in events no matter how distant and seemingly unrelated, how strong the bond between us and our first homes, first memories. Unbelievable, I thought too, how much I love the place I am from.

The Center of the Known Universe

"Well I was born in a small town, And I can breathe in a small town."

JOHN MELLENCAMP

Back Home Again in Indiana

THERE WAS ALWAYS the snow in the winter of 1980 and the frozen track where the horses bruised the soles of their hooves or burned the backs of their fetlocks. Before that time, I had never been further north with my horses than my home in the southwestern tip of Indiana, thirty miles away from the nearest racetrack in the state of Kentucky. I had come north instead of going south for the winter with my public racing stable because the old-timers said the pickings were easier at Hawthorne and Sportsman's racetracks. No one with really good horses that could win money in Florida, Louisiana, or Arkansas would be dumb enough to race in below-zero weather. "Go take the money from the fools," they said. And so I tried.

The thoroughbreds in my stable were good ones for the most part. They ran well during the race meet at Hawthorne Race Course. But I was a new horse trainer to this part of the midwestern racing circuit and, as such, didn't have the political clout or financial connections to be stabled in the limited barn area close to the track. The racing secretary gave me my own barn across the road at Sportsman's. That track was closed during the Hawthorne meet in November the way Hawthorne would be closed in December for the Sportsman's meet. Consequently, I had the whole racetrack to myself, not just the barn. I assumed, given the magnanimity of the racing secretary, I would get my own private barn again in December, but on the Hawthorne side. Resignation is an important aspect of life in thoroughbred racing. So I resigned myself to walking my horses across a busy asphalt road in subzero weather through a long tunnel to the paddock and, after each race, walking them back again.

I arrived in Cicero, Illinois, with my extended family, which included my wife, my four-month-old daughter, two of my wife's sisters who worked as grooms, a hot walker who had escaped from juvenile detention in Kentucky, and an exercise rider with aspirations of becoming the next Willie Shoemaker. We all lived in three separate dorm rooms above the stalls in our barn. The rooms were small and warm, with tiled floors and concrete walls painted a rotted peach color, and, once you got used to the constant smell of wet straw, horse liniment, and manure, quite comfortable. We slept on mattresses laid across the floor, and our only articles of furniture consisted of a used baby bed for my daughter and a black-and-white television set with a coat hanger for an antenna.

To a more civilized American, this may have seemed an impossible living arrangement, but we were racetrackers, a special breed of hardboots who were willing to sacrifice middle-class comfort for the adrenaline rush produced by hoofbeats thundering down the last stretch of sand and clay toward an invisible finish line and the winner's circle.

I liked Cicero. Once you got past the fact that it was a ghetto suburb of Chicago and had its own coterie of mentally deficient criminals, the city had much to recommend it. It was a tangible, cement manifestation of the yin and yang of life. For example, our first night there we parked our cars in the well-lit, well-guarded security lot next to the racetrack and walked up the block to a small, wood-framed building on the corner. It looked like any one of the dozen houses surrounding it, but was, in fact, Sporty Joe's Restaurant, home of the biggest beefsteaks in Illinois. The dining room was balmy, the waitresses friendly, the drunks happy, and the food delicious. I ate a twenty-ounce porterhouse steak that was so tender it sliced with a butter knife.

While we ruminated and meditated and drank a brandy with our coffee, a person or persons unknown removed the T-tops from my exercise rider's Camaro Z-28. In the same secure parking lot, a genius with a criminal mind that rivaled Lex Luther's broke the windshield out of my sister-in-law's car to steal her two-dollar St. Christopher medal hanging from the rearview mirror. He must not have been able to tell that the doors were unlocked in the shadows beneath the security lamp. As everyone surveyed the damage, I walked to the guard shack and asked the rather pleasant man hunched over an electric heater if he'd noticed anything out of the ordinary.

"No," he said, "just the usual run-of-the-mill vandals and car thieves."

"Did you try to stop them?"

"Oh hell no. Too dangerous."

"Did you call the police?"

"Phone's broke."

We retired to our rooms and considered the impracticality of driving a Z-28 without T-tops in the Lake Michigan winter. The next night my exercise rider left the keys in the ignition and, sure enough, the car was missing within a few hours. He called the insurance company and had the whole thing replaced much quicker than if he'd had to wait on new T-tops shipped from the factory.

* * * *

I made a lot of money that winter, just like the old-timers told me I would, but by January the horses were getting sore from running over frozen tracks. Hay prices soared to nine dollars a bale, which in 1980 was a fortune. The people around me developed a surly winter depression, and in the twenty-by-twenty-foot dorm room a virulent strain of cabin fever incubated.

My daughter, now six months old, cried most of every night with colic, or maybe she just vocalized a reflection of my own growing anxiety. Whatever was going on with her awakened in me memories of my own childhood. It hadn't been like this at all. I had an apple tree right outside my bedroom window, a huge backyard full of mystical promise, my own dog, a tricycle with red streamers on the handlebars, a mother who baked pecan pies frequently, and a father who had time to play catch every evening after work. Thinking about having all these things, I couldn't help but remember where I'd had them, on the corner of West Broadway and First Street in Princeton, Indiana.

If you had grown up like I did surrounded by corn and soybean fields, unencumbered by the labyrinth of streets and congested traffic common to Cicero, then you would understand my growing claustrophobia. If you had gone to schools where everyone knew your first name and no one carried weapons, then you could share my swelling anxiety. If you had ever slept with the doors of your house unlocked, ate fresh vegetables and unprocessed homemade ice cream, played baseball from the time you could crawl, and believed in Santa Claus, then you might sense how easily my memories soon developed a romantic, idealized impetus of their own. The misery of wintertime Cicero began to outweigh its financial possibilities in my mind. My daughter deserved better. My daughter deserved to grow up in a "special" place.

So I found a buyer for my horses and equipment. It wasn't difficult, and it didn't take long. The horses were worth the asking price, and I had always kept the saddles, bridles, and grooming gear in good shape. By the time the top layer of ice began to bead up and melt in Cicero, Illinois, I turned our old station wagon south and headed for Princeton, Indiana.

I can't say that I felt no regret. I loved working with horses, the freedom of being my own boss, the excitement of competition at a professional level, and a wad of money that belonged to just me bulging in my pocket. However, something greater than these sensory rewards and pleasures pulled at me. I had an overwhelming desire to give my daughter a real childhood, like the one I'd had. That desire required certain abstract, yet basic things—stability, security, joy, and love. All of these concepts could only be joined together and secured by a singular sense of place. And, for me, the world traveler, the gypsy, the vagabond, the Don Quixote in dungarees, any sense of place was centered in my memory of southern Indiana—home.

I have been back home again in Indiana since that January day in 1981 when I drove out the back gate of Hawthorne Race Course. I have changed jobs several times. I was blessed with a son in 1982 who, like my daughter, is now fully grown. My parents and several friends have died along the way. The Palace Pool Room and most of the retail shops that once surrounded the county courthouse in Princeton closed their doors years ago, replaced by video arcades, fast-food restaurants, and a Super Wal-Mart on the west side of town. And I have come to realize that my decision to return wasn't totally altruistic. Yes, both my daughter and my son got to know their grandparents, play Frisbee in Lafayette Park, own a puppy, join various youth groups, pick mushrooms, fish, and live in a real home. These proved to be good things for both of them.

On the other hand, I discovered that, for me, southern Indiana is an idea, an attitude, a memory, a sanctuary, as well as a location, created by my mind so I can handle the life that goes on outside and around me from the home I've built and love within me. It rides atop everything else in my mind like the needle on a compass and, when I drift too far from the path, it always points me back to "true" direction. For example, if my mortality begins to frighten me, there's a quiet spot on County Road 400 East in northern Gibson County, near the speck of a town called Wheeling, where I can park the car and hike across one of the last wooden covered bridges in the whole Midwest.

When I first walk toward it, the shape always seems unimpressive, a rectangle of rotted oak and pine, white paint peeling and flaking like snow in a slight breeze. The bridge is closed to vehicular traffic, and a new concrete and steel structure, heavy enough to hold the John Deeres and the grain trucks, bypasses it. But inside its loneliness, there is the comfort of time standing still. A small heart carved into a crossbeam traps two sets of initials separated by a plus and a date—May 1901. Tracing the scarred letters, I am transported back a hundred years when young lovers walked barefoot across the bridge, hand in hand, on the way to the one-room school in Mount Olympus, Indiana. The oil in my fingertips mingles with theirs, and I have spanned four generations in an instant. My fear of inevitable death is tempered by the fact that memories make us all immortal.

The southwestern tip of Indiana is also a wonderful place to learn anger management. If I'm late for work and find myself behind the most incredibly slow traffic in the whole world, it will be southern Indiana traffic, because here is a place where the expressways and parkways have traffic lights and on ramps that merge with off ramps. I relate this not as a negative, but rather as a positive. The crawl of my car between stoplights and the occasional locking of my brakes at an on/off ramp gives me the unique opportunity of running up behind a myriad of back bumpers pasted with wisdom: *Safe sex is in the palm of your hand; My wife says if she catches me fishing again she'll divorce me. Goddamn I'll miss her; God, Guns, and Guts made America. Let's keep all three; Your horn blows. Does the driver?; Illiterate? Write us for help.* It is impossible for me not to smile. I've obviously taken my time and myself much too seriously.

Do I ever wax nostalgic with fantasies of what might have been, of winning the Kentucky Derby or an Eclipse Award if I had remained hard at work on the racetrack? Of course I do. With his poem "The Road Not Taken," the great poet Robert Frost taught us that all men are prone to examine what could have been. But Indiana has surreptitiously supplied me with an answer for my occasional emotional longing. On Highway 41 South about four miles from the Evansville, Indiana, city limits, Ellis Park Racetrack rises from a soybean field.

Ellis was a family-owned enterprise for a century, but was recently purchased by the same corporation that owns Churchill Downs. And here's the neat trick. Until the last few years, wagering of any kind was prohibited by the Indiana state constitution. Ellis sits on the north, or Indiana, side of the Ohio River, which marks the boundary between Indiana and Kentucky, a state famous for horse racing and pari-mutuel wagering. A conundrum, you say. Not for the nineteenth-century legislators of Indiana. They simply passed a law that stated the Ohio River had changed its course after the famous midwestern earthquake along the New Madrid fault. The land, and only the land, owned by the Ellis family where the park stood was ruled by law to be part of the sovereign state of Kentucky. So I can legally go to the horse races and wager on my favorite steed while geographically never leaving Indiana soil.

It isn't necessarily the idea of gambling that brings me out to Ellis in the dog days of an Indiana August. It's the sights, the smells, the tastes, and the sounds. I love the taste of the homemade relish on the polish sausages. I hear the crowd rise to its feet on the balcony above me, screaming for one thousand-pound animal to stick his nose in front of another at an invisible wire on a clay track. I feel the ground vibrate as forty hooves drum down the stretch. For an instant, the air seems electric, swirling and crackling, like a jockey's whip has just sliced through it. The smell of leather and sweat is everywhere. I'm resurrected from normality by adrenalin.

That little dose of the past proves to be all I need. I see a family picnicking by the paddock, the children laughing as their father swings them around in the air. I say hello to people who live in my neighborhood or have been students of mine at the university. I talk with a father whose father bought a truck thirty years ago from my father or a woman who still remembers my mother's pecan pie. I bear in mind what brought me back to Indiana. I realize that when the last race runs, I have the quiet joy of getting in my car and driving *home*, and somehow that seems enough.

Saving the Dunes

ALONG THE BOTTOM CURVE of Lake Michigan, nestled between Gary's steel mills and Michigan City's utility company, lies a glorious and surprising area generally known as the Indiana Dunes. If you sit on the beach on a warm summer day somewhere in the middle, like where I live in Beverly Shores, and look straight ahead without turning your head to either side, you could easily convince yourself you were on some exotic island in the South Pacific.

In 1949 my father, a pediatrician, took a job at the Whiting Clinic. My parents had lived in New York City all their lives, and when they looked at Whiting, Indiana, on the map, they envisoned a lakefront beach resort with all the amenities. What they found when they got there was an oil refinery in their backyard, a soap manufacturer next door, and steel mills just down the road with all three billowing out huge clouds of smelly black smoke. My parents had moved to "Da Region," an unflattering term the rest of Indiana used to describe the Calumet Region, an area where fresh air was engulfed by smoke and the Little Calumet River flowed a sickly green with strange things floating in it that may or may not have once been fish. I had never heard the term "Da Region" until I went away to college in Bloomington and was bombarded with it every time I told someone I'd gone to Hammond High School.

I was two years old when we arrived in "Da Region," and from that age on, nearly every Saturday or Sunday of my life was spent in the dunes. My parents made the hour's drive the whole way on U.S. 12, leaving Standard Oil's big round tanks eastward through downtown Gary and Miller, after which the gray sky changed to blue and the concrete to sand. When I was in third grade, we moved from Whiting to Munster, now even closer to the dunes, and when I-94 was built, the drive was an easy thirty-five minutes. I had acquired a brother and sister by this time, and our childhoods were full of summer days at the state park beach, where there was ice cream and dancing at the pavilion; spring days climbing Mount Tom and learning to identify wildflowers; and fall days hiking the state park trails. My sweet sixteen party was a cookout at Wilson Shelter, where I would take my own children for their birthday cookouts years later.

How the Indiana Dunes and the steel mills came to be neighbors goes back to 1906, when U.S. Steel arrived. It was an ideal spot for a steel mill, providing nine thousand acres and seven miles of shoreline, with easy access to water and already-established rail transport. U.S. Steel engineers moved vast amounts of dirt and sand, diverted a river, built a tunnel into the lake, and built a breakwater using mountains of concrete and 160,000 tons of steel. The work was done with virtually no regulatory oversight. There was no such thing as environmental concerns in those days; land and resources were plentiful and seemingly inexhaustible. The Gary plant was seen as a step toward progress, bringing jobs and prosperity to the region, which it did for many years.

A half century later, Bethlehem Steel was built and was followed later by National Steel, Inland Steel, Midwest Steel, and the Port of Indiana. The dunes were getting eaten up, and the only part that was protected was the Indiana Dunes State Park, established in 1923 with funds raised by local garden clubs.

People began to take notice, in particular a sixty-five-year-old woman from Ogden Dunes named Dorothy Buell. Buell was an active clubwoman and an eloquent speaker. One day in 1952, she put up a sign asking for people interested in saving the remaining dunes from industry to come to a meeting at her home. A dozen women attended the meeting, and the Save the Dunes Council was born with Buell as its first president.

One day in 1960, my mother saw an ad in the Hammond paper advertising a Save the Dunes Council Dinner. She decided to go and see what it was all about and discovered a group of smart, intent, and well-organized people dead set on doing whatever it took to save the dunes from any further development. What they had in mind was a national park, a heady project for a group of regular people. There had actually been a proposal for a Sand Dunes National Park in 1916, but World War I put an end to any hopes of its passing.

My mother got involved. The Save the Dunes Council had a film called *Indiana Dunes: Playground of Mid-America*. She and others showed the film in hundreds of church basements and school auditoriums, anywhere they could find a captive audience. They spoke to community organizations and collected signatures on petitions. There probably isn't a person left in Lake or Porter County who hasn't been asked by my mother to sign a petition at one time or another. The Save the Dunes Council also had a newsletter, a well-written, interesting, and highly readable publication that got noticed. The council sought and received editorial support from newspapers across the country from the *San Francisco Chronicle* to the *Boston Globe*. The newsletter gained a lot of support for the dunes nationally, and the Save the Dunes Council became a force to be reckoned with.

The council also had the support of Illinois senator Paul Douglas, an influential man whose charisma and uncompromising convictions earned him a large group of loyal supporters. Many dedicated people worked tirelessly to save the dunes, but I think it's safe to say that the dunes would not have been saved without Douglas. Douglas grew up in rural Maine but by 1930 had spent ten years in the Midwest, teaching at the University of Chicago. He and his wife had a summer cottage in Dune Acres, and by the time he was a senator, he was a natural leader to join forces with the Save the Dunes Council after Indiana senators and representatives refused. Douglas was soon referred to as the "third senator from Indiana," and it was not meant as a compliment.

In the early 1960s my mother began going to Washington, D.C., to lobby for bills and to attend hearings with the Save the Dunes Council. She got to know our congressmen and anyone who could be influential on the dunes' behalf. On one memorable trip when the whole family went along, my brother and sister and I were in the audience when three astronauts were awarded Congressional Medals of Honor. We got to meet them and if memory serves, I believe the three were Alan Shephard, Scott Carpenter, and Gus Grissom.

While the building of U.S. Steel drew universal praise, the building of Bethlehem Steel in 1962 faced opposition, and it was the conservationists who made the difference. At the beginning of the century, when natural resources seemed endless, no one imagined the depletions that would be felt fifty years later—in fish, wildlife, and timber, not to mention water pollution.

From 1959 to 1966, Douglas tried to get bills passed for the federal purchase of land that would otherwise go to Bethlehem Steel. All in all, at least a hundred bills were presented. The battle between industry and conservation raged on, as some bills passed and some were defeated. Some land was saved, and many tons were bulldozed. As a teenager, I didn't pay a lot of attention to what my mother was doing, but I knew from her elation or tears which side was winning at any particular time.

In 1964 my parents built a summer home in Beverly Shores, and it was even a few years before this that my love affair with the dunes began to deteriorate. I was a teenager, and I had no friends in Beverly Shores. My friends were all in Munster, and I was not happy about being away from them just when the fun was starting. My brother was still young enough to be content with eating sand all summer, and my sister was not much fun either. We entertained ourselves by reading a paperback copy of *Father of the Bride* over and over again and waiting for friends to come visit. Once when there was an influx of dead alewives on the beach, I swore to everyone that they had died of boredom. But while my life was at a standstill, the battle for the dunes went on.

The fight for a national park was an interesting one because so many really powerful forces opposed it, among them the governor, the local congressman, industry, realtors, and the chamber of commerce. The dunes were essentially for sale, and everyone wanted a piece. But despite formidable opponents, it was for the most part ordinary people who favored a national park. Those who didn't want it were developers and local residents who didn't want their "private" beaches open to the public. But while the steel mills fought the park, oddly enough the steelworkers union supported it. Not only the steelworkers, but the AFL-CIO and the autoworkers as well. The labor unions were also strong supporters of Douglas, and they went to Washington and lobbied in favor of the park. This may seem a conflict of interest, but the union workers had a broader view of "just jobs." While of course they wanted and needed jobs, they were also looking at their quality of life. Even the "mill rats," as they were so pleasantly known, wanted their playground at the dunes.

It was a David and Goliath effort and a rare example of grassroots victory that in 1966 the National Park Service named the Indiana Dunes National Lakeshore as America's newest national park. My mother became the second president of the Save the Dunes Council that year and held the position for a decade. The council is now fifty years old and still going strong.

By this time I had graduated high school and had started college at Indiana University in Gary. During my freshman year, I made lots of new friends who were so impressed by my knowledge of all the back roads and places to hide out and drink beer in the dunes that I was always invited along to cut class and head for the beach. I had a boyfriend from Valparaiso, and suddenly Porter County didn't seem so bad. The next year I went to Bloomington, and after that my summers in Beverly Shores ended.

In the town of Beverly Shores, the park bought land that included many private homes. Needless to say, this caused problems. Homeowners had the option of moving the house or selling to the park and taking a twenty-five-year "leaseback," which meant that the park would own the house but the original owner could lease the house back for 1 percent of the sale price, which would be deducted at the time of the sale. The plan was that eventually the houses would be torn down. There was a lot of opposition to the buying and selling of leasebacks and even more in later years as new congressional committees passed different pieces of legislation that changed the leaseback provisions. Some leasebacks were extended to the year 2010. Some homeowners felt that the park's offers for their homes were too low or inconsistent. Residents did not want to move or to sell their homes to the park, and there was understandably a lot of hostility.

Congress carved up Beverly Shores based on the cost of acquiring the homes, leaving the bulk of homes within an area known as the "island," a large section of land that is surrounded by the national park but is not a part of it, thus bringing to the front a new battle: Town vs. Park. Although the park has been in existence for thirty-seven years, residents can still be easily identified as propark or antipark, and it is unlikely that the controversy will ever end.

Meanwhile, the Indiana Dunes National Lakeshore serves millions of visitors each year. Including the state park, there are fourteen thousand protected acres that include beaches, sand dunes, forests, wetlands, bogs, and prairies. Chellberg Farm and the Bailly Homestead, the first settlements in the area, are open to visitors year-round and are the site of the annual Duneland Harvest Festival, a weekend throwback to the nineteenth century that attracts more than fifty thousand people for the two-day event. I took my kids to the very first Duneland Harvest Festival when they were little, and there were about eighty of us there square dancing and eating corn on the cob. Campgrounds are full all summer, and the park's visitor center hosts a wide variety of programs all year. The park also contains a nature center and environmental learning center used by visitors and hundreds of schoolchildren on class visits.

The park is home to deer, fox, muskrats, beavers, rabbits, raccoons, and hundreds of species of birds. Even coyotes have been spotted. I've had deer on my front porch, raccoons and squirrels in the house. One summer day when I had the front door open, my then three-year-old daughter came into the living room to find three raccoons sitting on the sofa watching television. Her blood-curdling screams scared them off, but the squirrels were not so easily ousted; they broke a lot of stuff before finding their way out. The park is also a nesting area for the great blue heron and a stopping place on the North America fly-way path for birds traveling south. For one week each year, the sun sets behind the Chicago skyline, making for a spectacular one-of-a-kind sight. I've watched thousands of sunsets on Lake Michigan and have never seen the same one twice. The lake is also home to some strange optical illusions which I've seen but have yet to understand. Once in a while there are "inversions," where the Chicago skyline is seen plain as day but upside down. And there are rare evenings when the buildings across the lake look so huge and close, it's rather frightening. I've only seen this phenomenon a couple of times, and I have a friend who swears he saw the stoplights change on Michigan Avenue. I've also come to respect the dangers of Lake Michigan, as it can be as treacherous as it is beautiful. Shelf ice and riptides are familiar to the locals but have been the downfall of too many visitors. I've gone out in sailboats on clear calm days only to be pulled in by the Coast Guard an hour later under dark skies and large waves.

I left the dunes for ten years to go to school and see more of the world, but I came back to live and raise my children here. Thirty years later, I am still mesmerized by a sunset and delighted that I can come home from work, jump on my bike, and take a ride along the lakefront. I will never take it for granted. The uniqueness of the Indiana Dunes lies not only in its natural wonders and heritage and the fact that it lies between steel mills and a utility company, but even more so in the fact that it lies there at all.

A full and detailed account of how the dunes were saved can be read in Kay Franklin and Norma Schaeffer, *Duel for the Dunes* (Urbana: University of Illinois Press, 1983) and Paul Douglas, *In the Fullness of Time* (New York: Harcourt Brace Jovanovich, 1972).

Hoosier Crossroads

LAGRANGE, INDIANA, is a small, rural community in the northeast corner of the state, about eight miles from Michigan and thirty miles from Ohio. It's where I grew up, steeped in the ambience of mid-twentieth-century Hoosier culture. Even though Lagrange is the county seat, over time I have found it expedient, even necessary, to mention Shipshewana as a point of reference when telling someone about my roots. Shipshewana! In the days of yesteryear, Shipshewana was an Amish enclave consisting of a grain elevator on a railroad spur, a few stores, and a weekly livestock auction. Now you can go to Chicago or Detroit or Indianapolis or almost anywhere else and mention Shipshewana and people reply, "Oh, yeah. I've heard of Shipshewana." Not in my wildest dreams as a kid would I have believed that someday the Shipshewana livestock auction would transmogrify into an immense and immensely popular flea market and become a regular destination on the tour bus circuit. Nevertheless, it did, and that's where this all begins: somewhere near Shipshewana.

* * * *

I spent my childhood doing childhood things. I roamed the neighborhood with my friends and had free rein of the town on my bike. I read comic books and saved baseball cards that would be worth a fortune today if I had kept them. I went fishing in Fly Creek, baled hay for local farmers, competed in Pinewood Derbies, watched *Gunsmoke* and *Leave It to Beaver* and *Ed Sullivan* on black-and-

white television, survived yo-yo and hula hoop fads, put quarters in my penny
loafers, swiped cookie dough from my grandma's mixing bowl, went to drive-in
movies, and drank RC Cola on hot summer days. I spent hundreds (thousands!)
of hours playing baseball and basketball and army in the town park. The park
was an extension of my backyard, with only a narrow gravel lane separating the
two. A black cherry tree grew in the yard next to the lane, its upper extremities intermingling with the lower branches of an enormous ancient tree that
nobody could identify. It took three people holding hands to reach around that
tree, and its first limb was at least ten feet high.

One of my great early achievements, for which I received peer recognition
and accolades, was the discovery of a route that allowed my friends and me to
climb up the cherry tree, cross over into the "big" tree, and then keep on going
up until we were above the rooftops. From there we had a bird's-eye perspective
of the town. The least obstructed view was straight south, across the park. The
playground, basketball courts, baseball diamond, and quarter-mile cinder track
were all plainly visible. On the far side of the park we could see the row of trees
and bushes that formed a border along U.S. 20 and catch a glimpse of Fly Creek
as it flowed into the park through a culvert under the highway, then meandered
past the picnic pavilion before curving sharply and disappearing under the Canal
Street bridge. A few blocks to the west, beyond the railroad tracks, was the business district, where the courthouse clock tower appeared as a tiny spire extending
above the treetops in the center of town. The branches of that big old tree formed
a natural and well-concealed skybox, from which we surreptitiously kept an eye on
familiar streets, neighborhood haunts, and the rest of the known world.

And so I grew up immersed in the mostly simple, unexceptional pleasures
and adventures of youth, exciting only to the extent that an active, vivid imagination could make them so. Not everything was commonplace, however. Certain events and experiences intertwined to have a permanent, defining impact
on me. These were my Hoosier crossroads.

In the 1950s and 1960s, when I was growing up in LaGrange, there was
a stoplight at the junction of U.S. 20 and Indiana State Road 9. Big deal?
Well, yes—it was the only stoplight in the entire county. I rode my bike and
drove my car through that intersection probably thirty-eight million times.
You could say that it was the center of my microcosmic world. U.S. 20 began
in Boston and wound its way west for three thousand or so miles to its termi-
nus at Newport, Oregon. In the years of my youth it was a two-lane strip of
asphalt that spanned the continent and shared about a mile of its length with

Lagrange. It held the mystique of untold adventure as it stretched on forever in both directions, like Route 66. By contrast, Indiana State Road 9 offered little intrigue. It emerged from U.S. 31 east of Columbus and headed north to the Michigan line, crossing U.S. 20 by the Dairy Queen at the southern end of downtown. The day-to-day events of my childhood revolved about this hub. As a youngster I considered a few miles in each direction from the stoplight to be the edge of reality, beyond which lay the unknown. My world was indeed small, yet it was rich in life experiences and those intangible influences that make a person what he is.

* * * *

Indiana State Road 9 became Detroit Street as it ran through town. My dad and uncle owned a hardware store on Detroit Street, three blocks north of the stoplight. They went into business together following World War II, and Schlemmer Hardware became a fixture of the community. Creaky plank floors, open-bin seed displays, nails in wooden casks, pipe threading machines, the sound of a cutting tool striking a line on a pane of glass, and that distinctive smell that can't be described: that's how I remember the hardware. Oh, and the ancient, manually operated elevator that was used to bring stock up from the basement. I often stood on the elevator platform and took it up and down by pulling vigorously hand over hand on a thick rope that looped around a huge flywheel in the ceiling above the second floor. Between the ages of eight and about fourteen or so I worked at the hardware after school and on Saturdays, "elevating" stock, shelving merchandise, sweeping floors, and occasionally helping customers. But I never worked on Wednesday afternoons. Nobody did. For years the town's retailers followed a strange custom of shutting down at noon on Wednesdays. All of the stores closed. The hardware employees (that is, my dad and uncle) often went to Dave's Corner Bar for a "business meeting," during which they would drink a few longneck Blatz beers, discuss store issues, and solve any lingering world problems. They proved to my satisfaction that a carefully balanced combination of entrepreneurial gumption, dedicated hard work, and Blatz beer could ultimately pave the way to a successful business.

* * * *

I usually came into the hardware store through the back door, which provided entrance to the basement from an alley behind the store. Coming from
our home, I rode my bike up Spring Street, stopping at the Fly Creek bridge to
fling stones at a small island that was just within my range. Pretending to be an
air force bombardier, I allowed myself to continue my journey only after I had
struck my target five times, with the highest lobs representing the most devas-
tating strikes. From there, I rode over the railroad tracks and past the elevator,
where grain was loaded into train cars for transport to points unknown.

One time my mom and I were stopped at the railroad tracks waiting for a
freight train to pass when an Amish farmer who was leaving the elevator lost
control of his team of massive workhorses. They reared up, snorting and jan-
gling and straining against the wagon to which they were hitched, and I desperately fought a primordial, fear-driven urge to pee my pants as I watched their
huge flailing hooves crash down directly above my head onto the roof of the
car. In moments of crisis the brain enhances perceptions, and at that moment
I saw two colossal monsters with flaring nostrils and protruding eyes intent on
squashing a bug in their path. Unforgettable!

Anyway, from the grain elevator I rode on up the brick paved street and
turned left into the alley. The basement entrance to the hardware was where
semitrucks unloaded merchandise. Boxes of nails, paint, pipe fittings, tools,
and so forth were brought in the back door, loaded on the elevator, and hoisted
to the main floor. After parking my bike in the basement, I climbed the stairs
next to the elevator and entered the hardware via the plumbing section. Lots
of people used this way of coming into the store because their work trucks or
buggies could be conveniently parked in the alley.

The hardware store was a magnet for a cast of characters from the community. It drew farmers, mechanics, plumbers, electricians, carpenters, contrac-
tors, painters, and so forth, and it catered to the Amish population by selling
kerosene lanterns, leather goods, hand tools, buggy reflectors, and other items
that were of particular interest to them. This was a meeting place where gossip
was traded and politics and basketball were discussed. Small groups of Amish
would converse in their own brand of German dialect, completely unintelligible
to me. Men with crew cuts, dirty hands, rolled-up sleeves, coveralls, and steel-
toed boots would meet by the cash register and smoke cigarettes and share their
thoughts of the day. They'd kid me and make jokes that I didn't understand or
that embarrassed me, then they'd toss their cigarettes on the oiled-plank floor,
crush them with their boots, and head off to the next job. And I'd grab the push

broom and sweep up the butts as more customers walked in the front door and up from the basement.

* * * *

Two blocks further north on Detroit Street stood the stately red brick county courthouse, surrounded by streets of original bricks laid by hand around the turn of the last century. (My brother, who is on the town board, says that after tearing up those brick streets in 1999 to replace water mains and sewers, the board decided as a cost-cutting measure to pave them with asphalt rather than reusing the bricks. There was a revolt, resulting in a "Citizens' Brick Street Committee" that raised money to have the same bricks relaid. Thus, one can still drive on hand-laid, turn-of-the-century bricks in Lagrange.) The courthouse was topped by a four-faced clock tower with a bell that announced the time on the hour. One of my earliest memories is of the courthouse clock ringing the time in the middle of the night. It was a slow, mournful, familiar sound, resonating across the town like the chiming of a gigantic grandfather clock, and its echoing omnipresence made me feel somehow safe and reassured.

There was one night, however, when the ringing of the courthouse bell was not reassuring. That was the night the jail burned down. The jail was even older than the courthouse, which was built in 1878. It was a two-story brick building located across the street from the courthouse, and its interior burned with an unbelievable ferocity in the middle of a subzero January night. The entire town turned out to provide the volunteer fire department with hot coffee, blankets, and moral support. Water from the fire hoses froze on trees, on clothes, on the sidewalks and streets, on everything. The released prisoners teamed up with the firemen and policemen to fight the blaze, and it was a heroic, futile effort. The clock bell, almost directly above our heads, rang at midnight, and I remember its distressing, defeated sound. The men, including my dad and many others whom I knew and saw regularly in the hardware store, had lost the battle. Their clothes and faces were soot covered and ice encrusted. As the bell tolled, their efforts gave way to resignation and they, too, became spectators. I was very young, but something was instilled that remains today. My insular world had provided a compelling lesson about a community's response to disaster. The men I watched fight the fire were heroes in my eyes, and I saw the pride they had even in a lost cause. That lesson stuck and remains a part of me. I had reached a crossroads in my life.

* * * *

I reached another crossroads the following summer. A half mile east of the stoplight was the town park. A traveler leaving town on U.S. 20 would see it on the left, just past Canal Street. The park followed U.S. 20 for some way and large bushes, trees, and thick, tall weeds and grasses grew wild along the highway. My childhood friend, Roger, and I spent much time that summer masterminding and strategically constructing a series of "tunnels" among the trunks of the bushes and trees and through the weeds and grasses, so that we could crawl along the edge of the highway without being seen from either the road or the park. We played army in those tunnels, with headquarters at the picnic pavilion, and it was very adventurous and great fun. It was here that Roger and I saw a man die—or did we kill him? I'm still not sure. We were playing army on the banks of Fly Creek when we spotted a hitchhiker trying to get a ride out of town. We immediately realized that he was a Nazi saboteur (we always played World War II army) and that we needed to spy on him for the security of the nation. He was slowly walking along the road, stopping occasionally to put his thumb out whenever a car or truck came along. We could see that he was somewhat unsteady on his feet, and once he pulled a bottle out of his pocket for a drink, so it seemed pretty clear that he was drunk or close to it. We crawled through our tunnels as he made his way along the road, and so we stayed abreast of him, stopping when he stopped and moving when he moved. Our hearts were racing and the adrenaline was pumping. This spy was dangerous, our mission important!

Suddenly the hitchhiker decided to come over to the park. He left the highway and walked directly toward us. He was big and dirty and scary. Roger and I froze. If he kept coming he would literally stumble over us. And then with a great sigh he lay down on the ground with just a bush and some undergrowth between him and us, no more than an arm's length away. We could only see his feet and legs up to the knees. We were scared to move, but after a while he began to breathe steadily with a sort of snore so we thought he was probably asleep. Then Roger did the inexplicable. He reached out and grabbed the toe of the hitchhiker's boot. I don't know if Roger wanted to see if he was asleep or what, but whatever the reason, the man let out the most terrible gagging/gasping/growling groan that I've ever heard.

We were no longer immobilized, and both of us shot out of those bushes and made a beeline to Roger's house, where we told our tale to his mother. She called the police, and soon the sheriff came and picked us up so that we could show him where the man was. He drove us around to the spot and told us to stay in the car. Soon he returned and said gravely, "Boys, that man is dead." Heart attack? Alcohol poisoning? Massive stroke? Choked on something? Startled to death? Shot? Stabbed? Murdered? We didn't know and never found out. But we thought we had killed him, and so I began living with that belief.

* * * *

The jail fire, combined with killing a man in cold blood, left permanent imprints on my mind. My sleep was disturbed with nightmares of the dead man's face coming toward me, like Injun Joe in McDougal's cave, and then his scream and a feeling of panic. Occasionally that imagery was mixed with visions of flames leaping from windows and brick walls crumbling and vague shadows of grim, determined faces. I would lie there, listening intently for the court-house clock to reassure me that I was living in LaGrange, and that I didn't really kill anybody, and that just because the jail burned didn't mean that our house would, and that adults would take care of me even if they couldn't stop the fire or save a man's life. Hoosier crossroads. They could be very personal, but there were also forces and events outside my sphere of knowledge and experience that were slowly and in various ways intruding on my childhood.

* * * *

Six miles north of the stoplight, less than a mile from the Michigan line, was the East-West Indiana Toll Road. Ground was broken for the 157-mile toll road in September 1954, and it was completed and opened for operation in November 1956. During that time my family periodically got in our '49 Chevy and drove a few miles north on State Road 9 to watch the most amazing construction project ever undertaken in the county as it reshaped a swath of farmland to create a road like none other, an ultramodern superhighway. Every aspect of the project was accomplished on a huge scale. The earthmoving equipment and cranes were the biggest imaginable, the I-beams were longer, the bridge abutments were thicker, the road right of way was wider (much wider!), even the piles of dirt were higher than anything anyone had ever seen. Mom and Dad told us there would eventually be roads like that all over America. I remember Dad describing two wide, straight, unimpeded concrete lanes for each direction of traffic, something I couldn't fathom. He said that there would be restaurants and gas stations and bathrooms reserved just for people driving on the road, and that we could go to a White Sox game without ever stopping. My eyes widened in wonder at such visions. There was a big world out there, man, and things were happening.

* * * *

One night in early October 1957 my family went into our backyard and looked up into the heavens to watch a point of light dimly tumble and flicker across the sky against a backdrop of blackness and stationary stars. *Sputnik* was the first man-made object to be placed in orbit. Standing there next to the cherry tree straining our eyes to see an identified flying object in outer space felt very strange (alien, you might say), as if we were in a science fiction movie. We knew that the Soviet Union had accomplished this feat, that it was symbolic of our global competition with them and that we should be frightened by the Commie threat, but mostly we were just fascinated by the astounding human capability of tossing a 183-pound can beyond the grasp of Earth's gravity. So there I stood gazing into the night sky to see—what? The future. I didn't totally grasp the significance of the event, but I knew a threshold had been crossed. Occupying a tiny piece of ground in the middle of succotash country (nothing but corn and beans!), I unknowingly shared that moment with millions of other Americans as they, too, stood in their backyards and witnessed the birth of the space age. My final glimpse of *Sputnik* was framed by the upper branches of the big old tree. I guess our skybox provided a window that extended to realms beyond the known world, right into the Milky Way.

* * * *

There was a big world out there. Things were happening. Duck and cover was offered as an effective way to avoid serious injury during a nuclear attack. Polio was conquered through injections, then sugar cubes. A president was assassinated, followed by a civil rights leader and then the assassinated president's brother. The baby boom burst forth. A war raged in Southeast Asia. Riots erupted in urban streets. A man stepped on the moon. Rock and roll ruled. Yet in my secluded world with its center at the only stoplight in the county, there were constants that made change seem vague, far off, and not imminent at all.

One of those constants was the Amish. The Amish were a community within a community. I never quite understood them, although I had friends who were Amish. Lots of Amish children went to public schools until they could legally quit at the age of sixteen, and I had kids in my class named Yoder and Bontrigger and Stutzman and Miller and Hochstetler. Their speech was a little unusual because of the strong German influence in their homes, and their beliefs were different in a variety of ways, but many of them were excellent students (and strong basketball players, which always impressed me), and I pretty much took them for granted.

Amish country extended west and south of the stoplight; Shipshewana was eleven miles west on U.S. 20. Almost a third of the county had no electricity, and there was not an electric or telephone pole to be seen along those pastoral country roads. During my high school and college years I spent a lot of time in that part of the county working as a land surveyor. Twice while conducting farm surveys in the nonelectrified southwest, I witnessed Amish barn raisings. It was an incredible experience to see a full-blown barn materialize before my eyes in a day's time. The idealized images of many families gathering by buggy and the women preparing a banquet on expanses of picnic tables while the men with their hand tools and horses methodically construct a huge building—that's not a myth. That's really how it happened. Seeing it was like stepping into a Laura Ingalls Wilder story, momentarily making it feel like time had stood still.

* * * *

But time had not stood still. On December 1, 1969, I was in the television room of Owen Hall at Purdue University, watching with trepidation as Congressman Alexander Pirnie (R-NY) of the House Armed Services Committee began the selection process for a military draft. The Vietnam War needed more soldiers. Every eligible nonmilitary man in America born between January 1, 1944, and December 31, 1950, likely remembers that day. Pirnie reached into a large glass bowl and pulled out a small blue plastic capsule that contained a date. And with that, September 14 became lottery number 1. I breathed a quick sigh of relief, but knew that I still had to endure at least 125 more draws to make it past the projected cutoff.

As the drawing continued, my thoughts drifted back home again. I heard the slow, distinctive clop, clop, clop of a horse and buggy on a brick street. I couldn't get that sound out of my head. It called to mind a familiar scene that took on new meaning as I reflected on it. On Friday nights in the summer Amish teenagers traditionally brought their buggies into town and changed into "English" clothes in the public courthouse restrooms. They liked to gather by the massive Civil War cannon that was aimed at Detroit Street from the east courthouse lawn, eat Dairy Queen ice cream, and watch the toolers (high school boys in their cars) cruise endlessly around and around town trying desperately to see and be seen. I always thought there was something a little incongruous about a cannon with half a dozen Amish kids sitting on it. Now I saw the irony. Amish teenagers dressed in English clothes sitting on a cannon eating ice cream and waving to high school boys who would soon be shipping out to war. It was like they were waving good-bye, good-bye. . . . My reverie was interrupted when my birth date was called. I had drawn lottery number 131, putting me in a shadow world of uncertainty.

I was glad to be higher than 125, but I knew that even a slight escalation of the war would raise that upper limit, and I would be packing my bags for boot camp instead of transferring to Indiana University as I intended. I looked over to see how some of my friends had done, and the chair where one had been sitting was empty. I raised a questioning eyebrow at his roommate, and he replied by hooking his thumb over his shoulder. His birthday was September 14. The next morning he was gone, and I never saw him again. Hoosier crossroads.

* * * *

The crossroads of life are as personal as DNA, providing each of us with a unique set of lenses through which to view the world. No two people experience the same event in the same way, and nobody shares the same set of experiences with anyone else. Not to get too Zen about it, but in truth, every person's crossroads are different, and every moment is potentially a crossroads of one kind or another. Consider those two trees in my backyard. The black cherry tree was accessible, had plenty of branches, and was easy to climb, no ladder required. It was common, everyday, ordinary, mundane. As a child, my friends and I climbed up, around, over and among its limbs, and had a thousand moments that influenced our lives in mostly small, imperceptible, inconsequential ways. The "big" tree was different. It was inaccessible, imposing, overspreading; an unexplored wilderness. Even with a ladder, only the first limb could be reached, and that was a dead end: from there it was not possible to go higher. When I was little I looked into the midst of that wilderness from an upstairs window and dreamed of somehow transcending the cherry tree, of going beyond its limits and getting into the branches of that huge, inscrutable old tree. The secret of transcendence was revealed on that momentous day when I precariously scrambled and shinnied up a heretofore unconquered limb of the cherry tree and crossed the uncharted chasm. I was an explorer! A trailblazer! Making use of conveniently positioned handholds among the branches, I boldly made my way for the first time to the beckoning skybox and surveyed the known world through my newly acquired lens. And I liked what I saw.

Back Home on the Lakes

"LET'S TAKE A SPIN around the lakes," my father said.

It was yet another hot summer evening of my youth in our hometown of La Porte, just a stone's throw south of the Michigan border in the northwestern part of Indiana. There was no air-conditioning.

We piled into the car, our brand-new '57 Chevy Bel Air station wagon. Mom sat in the front with her window barely cracked open, afraid the breeze would mess up her hairdo. My sister, Renee, and I sat in the backseat while Dad drove, his right hand on the steering wheel and his left wrist resting upon the rearview mirror outside his open window. He turned the wing vent inward all the way so he could feel the wind upon his chest. He wore a thin, sleeveless tank top undershirt, an old shapeless hat, and a pair of baggy shorts. In the backseat, my sister and I cranked the windows all the way down and leaned out against the onrush of air streaming against our faces. We spit out a few mosquitoes as our car neared the lakes, but we didn't mind one bit. We were getting cooled off and that was what mattered. We hoped the drive would be endless, that it would take the whole night to get back home.

Dad drove quickly on the main streets of our small town to get away from the heat, but he slowed when we reached the lakes. As soon as we got a hundred yards off the main road, the temperature dropped dramatically. Now we were cool!

Dad drove easy around the lakes, some ten miles or so. All together there are seven lakes in La Porte, not counting ponds and backwater lagoons or swamps, though we usually cruised the main route around only Pine, Stone, and Lilly lakes. Renee and I listened to the crickets and frogs as we sat back and let the cool breeze waft over us. By the time we had circled the lake route twice, it was dark and almost chilly. Finally refreshed, Dad steered the Chevy onto the main road back through town, and we could now tolerate the heat reflecting off the pavement. After a few more blocks, we were starting to get warm again and begged Dad to stop at the Dairy Queen, pestering him for a large, double-dipped cone. He hemmed and hawed, giving us some excuse why we couldn't stop. Then, just as we were about to pass the DQ, our eyes ready to watch the ice cream stand pass behind us, he slowed suddenly and pulled into the crowded parking lot. We jumped out of the car and rushed to get in line. Renee and I each got into different lines to make sure neither of us was stuck behind someone ordering ten cones and four banana splits, some large request that would deter our advancement to the order window. We swatted mosquitoes as we sweated under the buggy neon lights and jumped to the window when one of us managed to get ahead faster. Dad was right behind us and paid for our orders while we ran back to the car and handed Mom her usual butterscotch-nut-dipped vanilla cone. We ate our ice cream in the car, wiping our lips with the crisp folded napkins Mom had insisted Dad bring. We licked first the melting cream that leaked from beneath the edge of the chocolate coating, then bit down upon the crunchy chocolate. We didn't notice the mosquitoes swarming in through the windows and could still hear faintly the bullfrogs bellowing from the lake in the distance.

Somehow the house seemed much cooler when we got back home, though the temperature inside had barely changed since we left. Dad had left the huge exhaust fan running in the upstairs bedroom. Left open also were the front and back storm doors, and the breeze rushed in through the screens. Still, it was warm in the house, but we were tired now and brushed our teeth before we went to bed. Though the nearest lake was but a mile away, Renee and I were lulled to sleep by the whirring of the fan and not the chirping of the frogs. No matter, we were asleep instantly, our mosquito-bitten cheeks still tacky from the ice cream cones and our skin still scented with the lake air.

* * * *

The nearest lake to my house was Clear Lake. It was less than a mile away, and I used to peddle there on my twenty-six-inch J. C. Higgins bike. In the basket across my handlebars were my trusty tackle box and a can of worms. I held my bait-casting rod and reel sideways with one hand while I steered with my other. When I got to the lake, I parked my bike against a tree and walked to my favorite fishing spot. The spot beside a weeping willow tree was also the site of my outdoor science laboratory, and I hoped to secure more specimens for my seriously important work in my basement lab back home.

More times than not, I backlashed when I cast and spent the next ten minutes untangling the knots in the reel. But I managed to get my line out fifteen or twenty feet from shore once in a while. Then, I watched for my stick bobber to dart under the surface of the water. When it did, I jerked my rod up sharply and set the hook into my prize, a lovely three-inch bluegill. If I were really lucky I snagged a small perch or rock bass. I carefully removed my hook from the gullet of each fish I caught and worked the clasp of the stringer through their gills, then slipped the stringer into the shallow water of the shore. When I had caught my "limit," or when it was suppertime, whichever came first, I raced home on my bike. I needed to get the fish safely alive back home, where I would immediately dump them, stringer and all, into the water in my mother's birdbath. The fish swam eagerly in the water, lapping up the goldfish food I sprinkled on the surface and bits of worms I dropped to the bottom. I needed healthy specimens for my experiments.

After supper I cleaned my fish with the Barlow knife my grandfather had given me for my birthday. I managed to get maybe a thin inch-long swath of flesh from each fish, which I proudly gave to my mother to cook for lunch the next day. But it was the fish eyes I was most interested in. I gently gouged each eyeball from the fish, but only after they were dead so as not to be cruel. I put all the eyeballs in an Alka-Seltzer jar I had retrieved from the trash behind the garage. When the jar was full of eyes, I poured rubbing alcohol over them and sealed the lid tightly. I carried the jar to my chemistry set in the basement. There, I placed the jars on the shelf next to my arrowheads and crinoids, small cylindrical fossils we called "Indian beads." Later, I would dissect the eyes, carefully peel the corneas away from the pupils, and remove the lenses. It was the vitreous humor I was interested in, the gooey liquid of the eyeball. I delighted in its viscosity for reasons I cannot remember, but I recall keeping dozens of jars full of fish eyes on the shelves of my lab, the older eyes bleached paler by their longer submersion in the alcohol. One special jar contained the tiny eyeballs of my sister's goldfish. I had bought it from her for a solid quarter, but when she learned what I had done to her pet, she cried for days. Sometimes I shook the jars and watched the eyeballs dance around inside, as if they were tamed monsters ready to regenerate into whole fish again were I to open the lids.

If I still had some time before Mom made me go to bed, I jumped back on my bike and took a spin around the lake just to look at the fishermen casting their lines out onto Clear Lake. I envied their catches of eight-inch sunfish and perch for the eyeballs of their fish, and I hoped to grow up soon, hoped to one day be big enough to dissect a man-sized catch.

* * * *

When the lakes froze during the winter, my father took me to the automobile races on Pine Lake. The snow had been plowed away into mountainous piles, and we stood in the infield of a half-mile oval and looked at the cars. They were mostly late forties and early fifties models, and their fenders were dented and scraped. When the cars spun around the oval their studded tires spewed a trail of tiny shards of ice. The plumes looked to me like the tails of comets I'd seen pictures of in my science book at school.

Of course the most fun was watching the cars skid around as they tried to pass one another. The cars bounced off each other's fenders as they raced, sometimes nearly locking bumpers. The cars didn't go very fast, but on the ice it seemed to me like they were speeding at a hundred miles an hour. Sometimes a car spun completely off the track and rolled into a snowbank. Then, the tow trucks pulled the cars from the snow and pushed the cars to get them restarted so they could rejoin the race. There were no seats for the audience, so we hopped from one foot to the next to keep warm. Some of the men in the audience smacked their lips when they sipped from their flasks, but Dad and I drank from his Thermos of hot, black coffee and ate thick ham and onion sandwiches. When I needed to pee, Dad told me to go behind one of the snowbanks, to where I had seen others trot earlier.

When the race was over, Dad and I walked back to land along the path. It started snowing hard, and our shoulders and hats soon became dusted with white powder. As we walked, he pointed out to me an old building on the shore. I had seen the front side of the two-story warehouse many times when we had taken a spin around the lakes in the summer. He told me the building was an icehouse and explained to me that before refrigerators, men carved huge blocks of ice from the lake and hauled them to the icehouse, first by teams of horses, then later by trucks. They packed the chunks of ice in straw to keep them from melting. That way, he said, people had ice all year round to keep their food cold at home in their iceboxes. How ice could withstand the heat of the summer in La Porte, when it often topped ninety degrees, mystified me, but I took my Dad's word on it. The best I could manage was to imagine that each of the blocks of ice kept its neighbor cold, somehow sharing their frozen body heat like I did when I snuggled up to Dad in the car before the heater warmed up the inside.

We got back to the car and Dad let the engine run a few minutes before we drove back home. A couple of inches of snow had already fallen, and it was coming down harder now. It was midafternoon on Sunday and already the sky was getting dark. Dad struggled with putting the chains on the tires, though I thought a few inches of snow was no big deal. I asked him why he was using the chains, and he said the storm looked like it could be a bad one and he wanted to have the chains ready to go for the morning when he drove to work. He worked in South Bend, about twenty-five miles away, at the Studebaker plant, and he told me the drive could be treacherous. When he finished buckling the chains, we got into the car, now warm, and took off our gloves so we could heat our fingers in front of the vents. Dad drove slowly on the way home through the snow and ice on the roads. Though we kept the windows closed, I could hear the clanking of the chains when we hit a dry spot on the pavement. By the time we got back home, it was almost dark, and, just for fun, Dad spun the tail end of the car a little bit for me when he pulled into the driveway.

* * * *

I haven't taken the car out for a spin in many years. I drive only with a purpose and destination in mind these days. Though I now live in Michigan, where it is difficult to be very distant from any kind of water, I don't drive around lakes on a summer night to cool off. Instead, I turn on the air-conditioning and shut the front and back doors of the house. I lock them after dark now, though we never did so when I was a kid in Indiana. I don't mind the droves of mosquitoes that haunt me at dusk, believing myself to have long since become immune to their venom. If I step outside to the screened porch on a hot summer night, I can listen to the frogs chirp in the distance and I get the taste for a double-dipped chocolate cone.

I quit fishing twenty years ago when it became obvious to me fish were not interested in my clumsy style of attacking the water with my rod. Nor, I learned, were the fish impressed with whatever bait I offered them. My last time fishing was during the spring perch run on a channel off Lake Michigan. The channel was only five or six feet deep, and I could see the perch easily as they swam along the bottom. The guy three feet to my left hauled them in every minute or two, as did the kid to my right. I, of course, watched as the fish nosed at my bait, refused to nibble, darted to the kid's bait, and swallowed it whole. When the kid limited out, he left me the rest of his bait, wigglers, he called them, and I tried again, even shifted position to my right so I would be exactly where the kid had been successful. Sure enough, the perch refused my bait and fairly leaped out of the water for the guy four feet to my right.

Snow has lost most of its magic for me since I have driven in it for thirty years during Michigan winters. To other drivers on the snow-covered roads, I must look like a myopic octogenarian as I creep ten miles below the limit on the highway to work. Long ago I added dying in a snowstorm car crash to my list of stupid ways to leave this world. (Among the others are snakebite, tainted oysters, and electrical shock from a home-repair job.) In the winter I drive only when necessary and keep my truck in four-wheel drive, unless the roads happen to dry out during a sunny spell. Cruising around in a snowmobile, something of a God-given right in Michigan, seems to me to be completely ridiculous. Often these snow bikes race along the shoulder of the road while I am trying to avoid death on the way to the grocery store, and I wish spring would come in February for a change. I'm certain one of these days some fool of a driver or kid on a snowmobile will dart into my path and I will spin out into a snow bank.

* * * *

I drive back home to Indiana several times a year to see my sister, Renee, and friends. She still lives in La Porte, though my parents are not alive, and the highway from Michigan enters my hometown at the northern edge of Pine Lake. While waiting at the stoplight, timed to turn red as soon as I arrive, I look out over the lake and remember the times we took a spin around the lakes to cool off. I remember the car races on the ice and the icehouse story my Dad told me. I think about Clear Lake, where I used to catch minnow-sized bluegills. Despite many new houses along the lakes and some commercial development on their shores, the lakes look the same to me as they did nearly fifty years ago. I'm sure I overlook much of the encroachment upon the lakes and see them as the waters of my youth. I like seeing my hometown in Indiana the way I remember it as a child. It's as if I know I could not be comfortable back home if I admitted too much change had tainted its lakes. In the thirty seconds I wait for the light to turn green, I think that the lives of the lakes are measured in millennia, while mine is in but brief years. Though it seems I have been on this planet forever sometimes, I also think I have been around only a minute or two, and have just barely enough time left to enjoy the lakes before I dry up completely.

The light turns green, and I cruise the back way around the lakes to my sister's house. In the summer I turn off the air-conditioning in my car and open all the windows so I can feel the lake breeze on me. I wear an old baseball cap, a sleeveless tank top shirt, and baggy shorts. I hang my left arm outside the open window and rest my hand atop the rearview mirror. I stop first at the Dairy Queen and buy a couple of double-dipped chocolate cones. I pull into Renee's driveway and park my car just this side of her concrete birdbath.

When I get to her house, we first lick the melting cream from under the edge of the chocolate, then we crunch the hardened coating. As we eat our ice cream she tells me she still hasn't forgiven me for dissecting her goldfish when we were kids. She laughs when I offer to give her another solid quarter for the fish, though I remind her I already paid for her pet fair and square.

When we finish, I ask her if she wants to take a spin around the lakes.

To Be a Native Middle-Westerner

"BREATHES THERE THE MAN, with soul so dead, who never to himself has said, this is my own, my native land." This famous celebration of no-brainer patriotism by the Scotsman Sir Walter Scott (1771–1832), when stripped of jingoistic romance, amounts only to this: Human beings come into this world, for their own good, as instinctively territorial as timber wolves or honeybees. Not long ago, human beings who strayed too far from their birthplace and relatives, like all other animals, would be committing suicide.

This dread of crossing well-understood geographical boundaries still makes sense in many parts of the world—in what used to be Yugoslavia in Europe, for example, or Rwanda in Africa. It is, however, now excess instinctual baggage in most of North America, thank God, thank God. It lives on in this country, as obsolescent survival instincts often do, as feelings and manners which are by and large harmless, which can even be comical.

Thus do I and millions like me tell strangers that we are Middle Westerners, as though we deserved some kind of a medal for being that. All I can say in our defense is that natives of Texas and Brooklyn are even more preposterous in their territorial vanity.

Nearly countless movies about Texans and Brooklynites are lessons for such people in how to behave ever more stereotypically. Why have there been no movies about supposedly typical Middle Western heroes, models to which we too might conform?

All I've got now is an aggressively nasal accent.

About that accent: When I was in the army during World War II, a white southerner said to me, "Do you have to talk that way?"

I might have replied, "Oh yeah? At least my ancestors never owned slaves," but the rifle range at Fort Bragg, North Carolina, seemed neither the time nor the place to settle his hash.

I might have added that some of the greatest words ever spoken in American history were uttered with just such a Jew's-harp twang, including the Gettysburg address by Abraham Lincoln of Illinois and these by Eugene V. Debs of Terre Haute, Indiana: "As long as there is a lower class I am in it, as long as there is a criminal element I am of it, as long as there is a soul in prison I am not free."

I would have kept to myself that the borders of Indiana, when I was a boy, cradled not only the birthplace of Debs, but the national headquarters of the Ku Klux Klan.

Illinois had Carl Sandburg and Al Capone.

Yes, and the thing on top of the house to keep the weather out is the ruff, and the stream in back of the house is the crick.

Every race, subrace, and blend thereof is native to the Middle West. I myself am a purebred Kraut. Our accents are by no means uniform. My twang is only fairly typical of European Americans raised some distance north of the former Confederate States of America. It appeared to me when I began this essay that I was on a fool's errand, that we could only be described en masse as what we weren't. We weren't Texans or Brooklynites or Californians or southerners, and so on.

To demonstrate to myself the folly of distinguishing us, one by one, from Americans born anywhere else, I imagined a crowd on Fifth Avenue in New York City, where I am living now, and another crowd on State Street in Chicago, where I went to a university and worked as a reporter half a century ago. I was not mistaken about the sameness of the faces and clothing and apparent moods.

But the more I pondered the people of Chicago, the more aware I became of an enormous presence there. It was almost like music, music unheard in New York or Boston or San Francisco or New Orleans.

It was Lake Michigan, an ocean of pure water, the most precious substance in all this world.

Nowhere else in the northern hemisphere are there tremendous bodies of pure water like our Great Lakes, save for Asia, where there is only Lake Baikal.

So there is something distinctive about all native Middle Westerners after all. Get this: When we were born, there had to have been incredible quantities of fresh water all around us, in lakes and streams and rivers and raindrops and snowdrift, and no undrinkable salt water anywhere!

Even my taste buds are Middle Western on that account. When I swim in the Atlantic or Pacific, the water tastes all wrong to me, even though it is in fact no more nauseating, as long as you don't swallow it, than chicken soup.

There were also millions and millions of acres of topsoil all around us and our mothers when we were born, as flat as pool tables and as rich as chocolate cake.

When I was born in 1922, barely a hundred years after Indiana became the nineteenth state in the union, the Middle West already boasted a constellation of cities with symphony orchestras and museums and libraries, and institutions of higher learning, and schools of music and art, reminiscent of the Austro-Hungarian Empire before the First World War. One could almost say that Chicago was our Vienna, Indianapolis our Prague, Cincinnati our Budapest, and Cleveland our Bucharest.

To grow up in such a city, as I did, was to find cultural institutions as ordinary as police stations or firehouses. So it was reasonable for a young person to daydream of becoming some sort of artist or intellectual, if not a policeman or fireman. So I did. So did many like me.

Such provincial capitals, which is what they would have been called in Europe, were charmingly self-sufficient with respect to the fine arts. We sometimes had the director of the Indianapolis Symphony Orchestra to supper, or writers and painters, and architects like my father, of local renown.

I studied clarinet under the first chair clarinetist of our orchestra. I remember the orchestra's performance of Tchaikovsky's *1812 Overture*, in which the cannons' roars were supplied by a policeman firing blank cartridges into an empty garbage can. I knew the policeman. He sometimes guarded street crossings used by students on their way to or from School 43, my school, the James Whitcomb Riley School.

It is unsurprising, then, that the Middle West has produced so many artists of such different sorts, from world class to merely competent, as provincial cities and towns in Europe used to do.

I see no reason this satisfactory state of affairs should not go on and on, unless funding for instruction in and celebration of the arts, especially in public school systems, is withdrawn.

Participation in an art is not simply one of many possible ways to make a living as we approach the year 2000. Participation in an art, at bottom, has nothing to do with earning money. Participation in an art, although unrewarded by wealth or fame, and as the Middle West has encouraged so many of its young to discover for themselves, is a way to make one's soul grow.

No artist from anywhere, however, not even Shakespeare, not even Beethoven, not even James Whitcomb Riley, has changed the course of so many lives all over the planet as have four hayseeds in Ohio—two in Dayton and two in Akron. How I wish Dayton and Akron were in Indiana! Ohio could have Kokomo and Gary.

Orville and Wilbur Wright were in Dayton in 1903 when they invented the airplane.

Dr. Robert Holbrook Smith and William Griffith Wilson were in Akron in 1935 when they devised the twelve steps to sobriety of Alcoholics Anonymous. By comparison with Smith and Wilson, Sigmund Freud was a piker when it came to healing dysfunctional minds and lives.

Beat that! Let the rest of the world put that in their pipes and smoke it, not to mention the works of Ernest Hemingway, Saul Bellow, and Toni Morrison; Cole Porter and Hoagy Carmichael; Frank Lloyd Wright and Louis Sullivan; Twyla Tharp and Bob Fosse; Mike Nichols and Elaine May.

And Larry Bird!

New York and Boston and other ports on the Atlantic have Europe for an influential, often importunate neighbor. Middle Westerners do not. Many of us of European ancestry are on that account ignorant of our families' past in the Old World and the culture there. Our only heritage is American. When Germans captured me during the Second World War, one asked me, "Why are you making war against your brothers?" I didn't have a clue what he was talking about.

Anglo-Americans and African Americans, whose ancestors came to the Middle West from the South, commonly have a much more compelling awareness of a homeland elsewhere in the past than do I—in Dixie, of course, not the British Isles or Africa.

What geography can give all Middle Westerners, along with the fresh water and topsoil, if they let it, is awe for an Edenic continent stretching forever in all directions.

Makes you religious. Takes your breath away.

Contributors

Pat Aakhus is the author of three novels, *The Voyage of Mael Duin's Curragh,* *Daughter of the Boyne,* and *The Sorrows of Tara,* published by Wolfhound Press, short stories, poetry, and a collection of essays. Originally from Los Angeles, she has lived in Indiana for more than twenty years and teaches creative writing at the University of Southern Indiana.

Leisa Belleau is a native of Newburgh, Indiana, a small town on the Ohio River, twenty-two miles from the setting of "Wish You Were Here." She is listed in *Who's Who Among American Teachers* and was nominated for the Associated Writing Programs Intro to Fiction Award while earning her MA in creative writing at Southern Illinois University. She has published poetry, fiction, and nonfiction in *The Southern Indiana Review* and *Public Conversations: Building Skills and Confidence.*

Ed Breen has been a journalist and historian in Indiana for forty years. A native of Iowa, he spent twenty-nine years as a writer, photographer, and editor at the *Marion Chronicle-Tribune.* He has been an assistant managing editor at the *Fort Wayne Journal Gazette* since 1995. He is a member of the Board of Trustees of the Indiana Historical Society and is a cofounder of the Mississinewa Battlefield Society. He attended Loras College in Dubuque, Iowa. He and his wife, Joanne, live in Marion and are the parents of two adult daughters.

Melanie Culbertson is assistant professor of English/creative writing at the University of Evansville and former fiction editor of the *Indiana Review*. Her stories have been published in *Puerto del Sol, Beloit Fiction Journal, American Literary Review, The Louisville Review, The Monocacy Valley Review, Wind*, and other literary magazines. In 2006 and 2004, she was nominated for a Pushcart Prize. She earned an MFA in creative writing at Indiana University, an MA in English at the University of Louisville, and a BA in English and journalism at Morehead State University. She is working on a novel.

Les Edgerton is the author of seven books, including the story collection, *Monday's Meal*, and *The Death of Tarpons*, which won a special citation of the Violet Crown Book Awards. His other books include three business books and a sports book he cowrote with his then-eleven-year-old son Mike. In 2003 he published *Finding Your Voice* from Writer's Digest Books (main selection, Writer's Digest Book Club). His short story, "In the Zone," was included in Houghton Mifflin's *Best American Mystery Stories, 2001*. Forthcoming is *Hooked: Write Fiction That Grabs Readers from Page One and Never Lets Them Go*, from Writer's Digest Books in Spring 2007, which will be a main selection of the Writer's Digest Book Club. Edgerton's work has been nominated for the Pushcart Prize, PEN/Faulkner Award, O. Henry Award, Edgar Allan Poe Award, Jesse Jones Award, and others. One of his screenplays was a semifinalist in the Academy's Nichol's Foundation Awards. He's been awarded two literary fellowships from the Indiana Arts Commission. A short story of his has been selected for the first (Spring 2006) issue of *Murdaland*. He is currently visiting writer-in-residence at the University of Toledo and also teaches writing online for Vermont College, where he received an MFA in Writing. He lives with his wife Mary and son Mike in Fort Wayne.

Rick Farrant is a thirty-three-year writing and editing veteran of newspapers and magazines, including the *Denver Post*, the *San Bernardino (CA) Sun*, the *Fort Wayne Journal Gazette*, and *Time* magazine. He has won numerous awards from the Hoosier State Press Association, Associated Press Managing Editors Association, and the Society of Professional Journalists. He has also guest-lectured on writing at a number of universities and has authored two plays and three books, including *Crossing Over: One Woman's Escape from Amish Life*. He was recently named Director of Marketing and Communications at United Way of Allen County in Fort Wayne.

Michele Gondi has lived in Mount Vernon since 2001 with her husband, Guillermo, and her children. Born in New York, she grew up in Argentina, where she worked as an elementary schoolteacher for twenty years. Also a ballet and theater instructor, she won the Alberto Closas Award for best director of children in Buenos Aires. She currently is a Spanish teacher in Mount Vernon and a ballet instructor in New Harmony. "The Redneck Gift" is her first publication.

Matthew Graham is the author of three books of poetry, *New World Architecture, 1946,* and *World Without End.* He is the recipient of an Academy of American Poets Award, a Pushcart Prize, two literary fellowships from the Indiana Arts Commission, a Maryland State Arts Council First Book Award, and a fellowship from the Vermont Arts Studio. Graham teaches at the University of Southern Indiana, where he codirects the RopeWalk Writers' Retreat and is poetry editor of *The Southern Indiana Review.*

Bill Hemminger teaches English and French at the University of Evansville. His poems, essays, and stories have appeared in many journals, including *Dominion Review, Under the Sun, Interdisciplinary Studies in Literature and Environment, The Formalist,* and *Evansville Review.* His academic work appears in *Southern Humanities Review, Research in African Literatures,* and *Présence Africaine.* He was a 1994 winner of the Syndicated Fiction Prize.

David Hoppe has worked as a public librarian, cultural administrator, and creative advertising consultant since moving to Indiana in 1988. He currently serves as associate editor for *NUVO,* the alternative weekly in Indianapolis. Hoppe holds an MA in library science from the University of Minnesota and an MFA in creative writing from Bennington College. In 1989 he edited *Where We Live: Essays about Indiana,* which was published by Indiana University Press. He has published fiction, nonfiction, and poetry and is now working on a play. His work can be found at www.davidhoppewriter.com.

Terry Kirts teaches in the Department of English at Indiana University—Purdue University in Indianapolis. He holds an MFA in creative writing from Indiana University, Bloomington, where he studied on a Ruth Lilly Fellowship. His poems have appeared in such publications as *Another Chicago Magazine, Crab Orchard Review, Gastronomica, Green Mountains Review, Maize, Third Coast, Artful*

Dodge, and *The James White Review*, as well as the anthologies, *This New Breed* and *Food Poems*. His essays have appeared in *The Drexel Online Journal*, and his restaurant reviews and culinary articles have appeared in *NUVO, Dine, Indianapolis Woman*, and *WHERE Indianapolis*.

Michael Martone is the author of *Alive and Dead in Indiana, Fort Wayne Is Seventh on Hitler's List, The Blue Guide to Indiana, Michael Martone*, a memoir made up of contributor's notes, *Unconventions*, a book on writing, and *Rules of Thumb*, edited with Susan Neville. He is the editor of *A Sense of Place: Essays in Search of the Midwest* and *Townships*. He teaches creative writing at the University of Alabama.

Jim McGarrah is an Indiana native. He has been managing editor of the national literary magazine *The Southern Indiana Review* since 1998 and teaches creative writing at the University of Southern Indiana. He codirects the Rope-Walk Readers Series and serves on the RopeWalk Writers Retreat staff in New Harmony, Indiana, as well as the New Harmony Arts Committee. In addition, McGarrah is an award-winning poet and essayist whose most recent works have been published in *Café Review, Cedar Hill Review, Connecticut Review, Elixir Magazine, North American Review*, and *Under the Sun*. McGarrah's first book of poetry, *Running the Voodoo Down*, won the Editor's Choice Prize from Elixir Press and was published by them in 2003. His memoir, *A Temporary Sort of Peace*, about his experiences as a combat Marine in Vietnam will be published by the Indiana Historical Society Press in 2007.

Margaret McMullan is the author of four novels, *How I Found the Strong, In My Mother's House, When Warhol Was Still Alive*, and the forthcoming *Crossing No Bob*. Her essays and short stories have appeared in *Glamour*, the *Chicago Tribune, Southern Accents*, the *Indianapolis Star, TriQuarterly, Michigan Quarterly Review, The Greensboro Review, The Southern California Anthology*, and *Boulevard* among others. In 2005 McMullan won the Mississippi Institute of Arts & Letters Award for Fiction and Southwestern Indiana's Arts Council Award for Artist of the Year. *How I Found the Strong* won the Indiana Best Young Adult Book of Fiction 2004. Her radio commentaries can be heard frequently on WNIN radio and NPR affiliates. She received a Special Mention in the 2006 Pushcart Prize collection and two Individual Artist Fellowships from the Indiana Arts Commission and the National Endowment for the Arts. McMullan received her MFA in fiction from the University of Arkansas, Fayetteville, and she is a professor of English at the University of Evansville in Evansville, Indiana. She is currently working on her fifth novel.

Susan Troy Meyer writes book reviews for the *Michigan City News-Dispatch*. Her weekly column, "Cause I Said So, That's Why," a humorous column on parenting, ran in the *News-Dispatch* for ten years, with reprints published in three other papers: *Parent's Press* in Berkeley, California; *Child Times* in Birmingham, Alabama; and *Colorado Parent* in Denver, Colorado. She has published in *The Sun*, a literary magazine from the University of North Carolina. She was also editor of and contributor to her town paper, the *Beverly Shores Newsletter*, for two years. Besides writing, she is a yoga instructor and the graphics coordinator for the Michigan City Public Library.

Alyce Miller, who came to Indiana eleven years ago from San Francisco, now leads a double life as a full-time writer and a professor in the English Department at Indiana University at Bloomington and a part-time attorney specializing in animal rights. Her novel, *Stopping for Green Lights*, was published by Anchor Doubleday, and her collection of stories, *The Nature of Longing*, won the Flannery O'Connor Award for Short Fiction. She has published numerous stories, essays, poems, and articles in such magazines as *The Sun*, *The Iowa Review*, *Glimmer Train*, *Story Quarterly*, *Fourth Genre*, *Chicago Tribune*, *New England Review*, *Michigan Quarterly Review* (Lawrence Prize), and *Kenyon Review* (Kenyon Review for Literary Excellence in Fiction Prize).

Deborah Zarka Miller teaches creative writing, literature, and composition at Anderson University. She also serves as director of the university's Writing Lab and faculty adviser for *Literary Arts* magazine. In November 2005 she completed an MFA in writing from Spalding University and finished her first young adult novel. Her current writing projects include picture book texts and an adult novel. In addition to Miller's work at Anderson University, she conducts writing workshops at churches in central Indiana and serves extensively in the children's ministries of her home church. Miller and her husband live in Anderson with their daughter and two sons.

Susan Neville is a lifelong resident of Indianapolis. Her books include *Indiana Winter*, *In the House of Blue Lights* (Richard Sullivan Prize for Fiction), *The*

Invention of Flight: Stories (Flannery O'Connor Award for Short Fiction), *Iconography: A Writer's Meditation, Fabrication: Essays on Making Things and Making Meaning,* and *Twilight in Arcadia: Tobacco Farming in Indiana.* Her work has appeared in *The Georgia Review, North American Review,* and *The Pushcart Prize Anthology.*

Scott Saalman is the manager of employee communication for Kimball International in Jasper, Indiana. His fiction has appeared in *The Southern Indiana Review, The Flying Island,* and the *Herald,* a newspaper in Dubois County.

Born in Tennessee and reared in Ohio, Scott Russell Sanders studied in Rhode Island and Cambridge, England, before going on to become a Distinguished Professor of English at Indiana University. Among his more than twenty books are novels, collections of stories, and works of personal nonfiction, including *Staying Put, Hunting for Hope,* and *A Private History of Awe.* His writing has won the AWP Creative Nonfiction Award, the John Burroughs Essay Award, and the Lannan Literary Award. He and his wife, Ruth, a biochemist, have reared two children in their hometown of Bloomington in the hardwood hill country of Indiana's White River Valley.

Phil Schlemmer grew up in Lagrange, Indiana, and now lives in Grand Rapids, Michigan, with his wife and daughter. He has been a teacher, writer, and educational consultant and is currently Curriculum Director for Holland Public Schools in Holland, Michigan. He has published numerous articles in educational journals and elsewhere and has won a Teachers' Choice Award from *Learning* magazine for his 1999 book *Challenging Projects for Creative Minds.* He has published eight textbooks containing creative, challenging curricula. His forthcoming book, *Balancing the Classroom,* is scheduled for publication in early 2007.

Kurt Vonnegut was born in Indianapolis. In 1996, after the publication of *Timquake,* he announced his retirement from writing fiction. *A Man Without a Country* (2005) is a collection of recent essays first appearing in *In These Times,* an independent magazine of politics and culture. Perhaps best known for his novel, *Slaughterhouse-Five,* he has written thirteen other novels, including *Cat's Cradle* and *Hocus Pocus.* His three collections of short stories are *Canary in a Cathouse, Welcome to the Monkey House,* and *Bagumbo Snuff Box.* He has written five plays, including *Happy Birthday, Wanda June,* five collections of essays, including

Wampeters, Foma and Granfalloons, and seven film adaptations, including *Breakfast of Champions.* Vonnegut remains America's premiere man of letters.

Tom Watson was born and raised in La Porte, Indiana. He is an online adjunct instructor of creative writing for Indiana University and recently retired from teaching writing for thirty years to at-risk populations for the Grand Rapids Public Schools. He has been an associate editor for *The Crescent Review* and a contributing editor for *Hunger Mountain,* the Vermont College journal of arts and letters. His short story collection, *See Rock City and Other Stories,* placed as a semifinalist in the 2001 Julia Peterkin Prize competition. His essays have appeared in *Peninsula: Essays and Memoirs from Michigan, Those Who Do, Can: Teachers Writing, Writers Teaching,* and elsewhere. His fiction has appeared in *The Southern Indiana Review, Ellipsis: Literature and Art,* and numerous other journals and has been nominated for a Pushcart Prize. He received his MFA in writing from Vermont College and lives near Grand Rapids, Michigan, with his wife, Tam Bagby. He is currently at work on a memoir about his teaching career.

Tom Wilhelmus is the former dean of the School of Liberal Arts at the University of Southern Indiana and former chair of the Indiana Humanities Council. He is founder and codirector (with poet Matthew Graham) of the RopeWalk writers Retreat in New Harmony and senior editor of *The Southern Indiana Review.* He holds a PhD in literature from the University of Notre Dame and has been a regular contributor to *The Hudson Review* in New York, where he publishes articles on contemporary fiction. He teaches graduate courses in liberal studies and contemporary literature.